J. WESTON
WALCH
PUBLISHER
Portland, Maine

Content-Area Reading Strategies

Social Studies

Lisa French

User's Guide
to
Walch Reproducible Books

Purchasers of this book are granted the right to reproduce all pages where this symbol appears.

This permission is limited to a single teacher, for classroom use only.

Any questions regarding this policy or requests to purchase further reproduction rights should be addressed to:

Permissions Editor
J. Weston Walch, Publisher
321 Valley Street • P.O. Box 658
Portland, Maine 04104-0658

Contents

INTRODUCTION
To the Teacher

Content-Area Reading Strategies teaches students how to read to learn. In the early grades, students learn to read and write narratives—stories. They are used to dealing with texts that have a beginning, a middle, and an end. They expect to encounter rising action that leads to a climax and then to a resolution.

This pattern of organization is often not followed in informational texts, which begin to make up a large portion of classroom-related reading about grade four. Without instruction in how to read these kinds of nonnarrative texts, even "good" readers can stumble. Some research shows that the so-called "fourth-grade reading slump" may be attributable in part to the unsupported transition from narrative to informational texts.

That's where the *Content-Area Reading Strategies* series comes in. Each book in the series focuses on a different content area, and gives students concrete tools to read information texts efficiently, to comprehend what they read, and to retain the information they have learned.

Organization is an important part of comprehending and retaining knowledge. The graphic organizers in *Content-Area Reading Strategies* help students connect new information to their existing schemata, increasing their ability to recall and take ownership of what they read. The reading strategies give students a way to "see" what they read—a great asset to visual learners.

The reading-writing connection is a strong one. The reading strategies in this book all require students to record information in writing, strengthening readers' ability to retain and access newly acquired knowledge.

Classroom Management

Content-Area Reading Strategies is easy to use. Simply photocopy each lesson and distribute it. Each lesson focuses on a single strategy and includes models showing the strategy in action. At the back of this book, there are blank copies of each graphic organizer, so you can copy them as often as needed. Quiz questions assess how well students understood what they read.

The Practice Readings provide longer readings and questions. For these, you may want to let students choose which strategy to use, or you may assign a particular strategy. Either way, have copies of the appropriate graphic organizers available.

Eventually, students will no longer need printed graphic organizers; they will make their own to suit their learning style and the particular text they are reading. They will have integrated the reading strategies as part of the learning process in all content areas.

INTRODUCTION
To the Student

Welcome to *Content-Area Reading Strategies!* This book will give you the tools you need to read, understand, and retain the texts you read for school. These strategies will save you time by helping you to extract information efficiently from your reading, to organize that information so that it is easy to understand, and to remember the information through writing it.

You may have heard about the writing process—the steps you follow to write a paper, letter, story, or anything else. But did you know there is also a reading process?

The reading process consists of three major steps: prereading (before reading), during reading (the reading itself), and postreading (after reading.) This book gives you specific strategies to use to accomplish each step. These strategies are given form in graphic organizers, which ask you to think and write about your reading. Breaking up a big task, such as reading a whole social studies chapter, into smaller steps makes the job easier to tackle. These graphic organizers make studying for tests less stressful, too—all the information is already written down in a condensed form, in your own words. No more last-minute cramming!

Everyone reads and learns differently, and you will probably find that some strategies are more helpful to you than others. Give them all a try, and find out what works for you. Customize the strategies to your way of reading and learning. Eventually, you will not need the printed graphic organizers at all. You'll follow the reading process steps automatically and organize the information in the way most meaningful to you.

PART I
Building Vocabulary

LESSON 1
Using Context Clues

Building Vocabulary

Reading can be a complex process. Whenever you read, you apply decoding skills of various kinds to get meaning from the text. One of those skills—and a vital one—is recognizing and understanding vocabulary.

Vocabulary is the collection of words that you encounter throughout your reading life. In fact, the English language is so rich with words that your vocabulary will probably continue to grow for as long as you continue to read. Increasing your vocabulary will not only make you sound more articulate when you write and speak, it will also increase your understanding of anything else you read and hear.

No matter what you're reading—a textbook, a newspaper article, a popular magazine, a Web page, or the liner notes for some new music—you will understand and appreciate it more if you know what each word means. How can you make this happen?

Strategies to Use

Here are some of the most effective ways to build vocabulary as you read:
- Analyzing context clues
- Recognizing word parts like prefixes and suffixes
- Looking for words within words

Let's take a look at the first strategy listed above — analyzing context clues.

Analyzing Context Clues

What does the phrase *context clues* mean? Context clues are the parts of a reading that surround a word or phrase you don't know and that can shed some light on its meaning. Some examples of context clues might be
- a definition before or after the unfamiliar word or phrase
- a synonym or an antonym near the unfamiliar word
- examples in the text that illustrate the meaning of the unfamiliar word or phrase
- restatement of the basic meaning of the unfamiliar word or phrase

Using Context Clues *(continued)*

Context Clues in Action

Read the following passage.

The husband of Loreta Velázquez had always <u>vacillated</u> about which side he should take in the Civil War. He was born in Texas, which was part of the South. Like many other Southerners in the U.S. Army, he was divided between loyalty to the Union, which gave him his career, and his family's <u>allegiance</u> to the Confederate South. He wavered between the two sides. Velázquez, having been raised in the South, convinced her husband to quit his job with the Union army and join the Confederate army. As soon as he went east to begin training for battle, she formed a plan to join him. Since women were <u>prohibited</u>— forbidden by law—to be soldiers, she decided to disguise herself as a man.

Velázquez went to New Orleans in early 1861 to carry out her plan. First, she had a tailor sew a special padded uniform that made her waist appear larger and more masculine. Then she had a barber cut and style her hair to resemble that of a man. Next, a trusted male friend helped her glue on a false mustache. He also helped her practice disguising her voice and feminine <u>mannerisms</u>, like tossing her head and taking short, dainty steps. Finally she selected the name Lieutenant Harry T. Buford, CSA. The transformation was complete.

Adapted from *Latino Heroes of the Civil War* by Michael Walbridge. ©1997 by J. Weston Walch, Publisher.

In this passage, some challenging words have been underlined. At first glance, these words may appear baffling. However, you can begin to make sense of them by analyzing context clues. The following is an example of how you might use context clues to figure out the meaning of new words.

The first underlined word, *vacillated*, is not defined or explained in the sentence in which it occurs. But I see that the next two sentences restate *vacillate's* meaning: Velazquez's husband "was divided" between loyalty to the North (the Union) and the South (the Confederates). He "wavered" between the North and the South. Let me try substituting "was divided" or "wavered" for *vacillated*. That works! "The husband of Loreta Velazquez had always been divided about which side he should take in the Civil War." Now I know that *vacillated* means "felt divided" or "wavered between."

The next underlined word is *allegiance*. In the first part of the sentence, I see what looks like a related phrase: "he was divided between loyalty to the Union . . . and his family's allegiance to the Confederate South." The related term for *allegiance* is *loyalty*; I think they are synonyms.

Using Context Clues *(continued)*

Prohibited, the next underlined word, is actually followed by a definition: forbidden by law.

The fourth underlined word, *mannerisms,* is followed by a couple of examples: "like tossing her head and taking short, dainty steps." These are examples of ways of moving—gestures—that are sometimes considered typically feminine. Maybe *mannerisms* means "typical gestures or habits."

Application

Read the following passage. Then use what you have learned about context clues to answer the questions.

Samuel Adams was born in Boston in 1722. His father, also named Samuel, was a wealthy businessman and an important figure at the Old South Meetinghouse and thus was referred to as Deacon Adams. At fourteen, young Samuel Adams entered Harvard, as expected of the son of a Boston <u>dignitary</u>. There are no records of his academic career, but it is probable that at Harvard Adams became familiar with John Locke's powerful written argument *Of Civil Government.* In this <u>treatise</u>, Locke set out his <u>doctrine</u> that every citizen had natural rights of life, liberty, and property. This position also meant that a ruler could not take property from his or her subjects in the form of taxation without their consent.

Adams graduated from Harvard in 1740 and went on to receive his master's degree in 1743. In 1748, Deacon Adams died, and Samuel inherited his father's business, which supplied malt to brewers. Under Samuel's control the business soon began to weaken, then to fail. What really came to interest Samuel Adams was politics. By 1763, he had joined the <u>Caucus</u> Club. This was a secret organization that met in advance of all town meetings to decide upon the slate of candidates for office and what the stands would be on various issues.

Adapted from *Critical Thinking Using Primary Sources in U.S. History* by Wendy S. Wilson and Gerald H. Herman. ©2000 by J. Weston Walch, Publisher.

1. Based on your reading of context clues, how would you define the word *dignitary*?

   What examples can you find in the reading to support your definition?

2. How would you define *treatise*?

   What context clue helped you in your definition?

3. How would you define *doctrine*?

   What context clue helped you in your definition?

4. How would you define *caucus*?

   What context clues helped you in your definition?

LESSON 2
Prefixes and Suffixes

In Lesson 1, you learned how to use context to work out the meaning of unfamiliar words. Another good way is to look for a prefix or suffix that can help you decode the word's meaning. Prefixes and suffixes are attached to the central "core" or root of many words of more than one syllable.

Prefixes

Prefixes are word parts that are found at the *beginning* of words. The prefix *pre-* means "before" or "beginning."

Here are some common prefixes to watch for as you read.

Common Prefixes			
ab-	from, off	intra-	within
ad-	to, toward	magn-	large
anti-	against	micro-	small
auto-	self	non-	not
bi-	two	pre-	before
con-	with	pro-	for, in favor of
contra-, counter-	against, opposite	re-	again
dis-	not	sub-	under, below
ex-	out from OR no longer	super-	above
extra-	beyond	sym-	together
im-	not	tri-	three
in-	into OR not	un-	not
inter-	between, among	uni-	one

Examples

- *The United States is <u>bisected</u> by the Mississippi River.*
  You know that the prefix *bi-* means "two," so you can make an educated guess that this word means "divided into two sections."
- *One of the goals of Dr. Martin Luther King, Jr. was <u>interracial</u> harmony.*
  You know that the prefix *inter-* means "between" or "among," so you can make an educated guess that this word means "between races."

Prefixes and Suffixes *(continued)*

Suffixes

Suffixes are word parts that are found at the end of words. Here are some common suffixes you can learn to recognize in your reading.

Common Suffixes			
-able, -ible	able to be	-less	without
-ful	full of	-ly	in such a manner
-hood	condition, state	-ment	state; act
-ion, -tion,		-ship	state, condition
-ity	state; quality	-some	like, tending to
-ish	like; having the characteristics of	-ward	in the direction of
-ive	relating to; having the quality of		

Example

- *The crew of the clipper ship spotted land to the <u>windward</u> side.*
  Since *-ward* is a suffix meaning "in the direction of," you can assume that the crew saw land in the direction from which the wind was blowing.

Prefixes and Suffixes in Action

Read the following passage.

> In November 1753, George Washington was asked by the governor of Virginia to investigate the newly built French forts along the Ohio River and to ask the French to withdraw. Washington met with many difficulties along the way, including <u>impassable</u> streams and <u>bothersome</u> weather.
>
> When he finally met with the French, Washington commented, "They pretend to have an <u>undoubted</u> right to the river from a discovery made by one La Salle sixty years ago." His <u>counterproductive</u> discussions with the French eventually led to the beginning of the Seven Years War.

The underlined words in the paragraph above may be unfamiliar to you. Your knowledge of prefixes and suffixes can help you decode them. Take the word *impassable*, for instance. It consists of three parts: the prefix *im-* ("not"), the core word *pass* ("to go by or over"), and the suffix *-able* ("able to be"). If you put all three of these meanings together, you get "not able to be passed or crossed over." In other words, Washington found many streams that he could not cross.

Prefixes and Suffixes *(continued)*

The word *bothersome* consists of the core word *bother* ("to worry, trouble, or annoy") and the suffix *-some* ("tending to"). Poor weather tended to bother the travelers in Washington's party.

What about *undoubted*? Take the prefix *un-* ("not") and the familiar word *doubted*. The meaning of this word is "not doubted," or "certain."

Finally, take the word *counterproductive*. The prefix *counter-* means "against" or "the opposite of." The core word *product* means "effect" or "result." The suffix *-ive* means "having the quality of." Taken as a whole, this word means that Washington's discussions with the French were the opposite of having a good effect—they did not have a positive result.

Application Read the passage below. Then use your knowledge of prefixes and suffixes to answer the questions that follow.

In 1848 and 1849, the gold rush lured thousands of fortune hunters from all over the world to California. In a number of <u>uninhabited</u> wilderness areas, one canvas city after another sprang up nearly overnight. In places like Sacramento and Stockton, men dug <u>feverishly</u> for the <u>subterranean</u> gold dust that could bring up to five hundred dollars a day for the lucky. However, once the gold was <u>extracted</u> from the earth and sold, many fortunes were foolishly lost through drinking, gambling, horse trading, and other wild behavior. There was a general feeling that the gold supply would last forever. As one prospector wrote of his fellow diggers, "They had found gold at every step and looked on the supply as <u>inexhaustible</u>." Of course, this assumption was proved wrong in the years that followed.

1. The word *uninhabited* means
   (a) not occupied
   (b) not behaving in a socially acceptable way
   (c) crowded
   (d) not having a regular routine
   Which vocabulary strategies helped you figure out the meaning of this word? _____

   _____

Prefixes and Suffixes *(continued)*

2. *Feverishly* means
   (a) at a reasonable pace
   (b) in high temperatures
   (c) with intensity
   (d) with little hope
   Which vocabulary strategies helped you figure out the meaning of this word? _____

   _____

3. *Subterranean* refers to something that is
   (a) under the sea
   (b) under the earth
   (c) in a ship
   (d) hidden in a tunnel
   Which vocabulary strategies helped you figure out the meaning of this word? _____

   _____

4. The word *extracted* means
   (a) blown up
   (b) sold
   (c) moved on tracks
   (d) removed
   Which vocabulary strategies did you use? _____

   _____

5. *Inexhaustible* describes something that is
   (a) not causing pollution
   (b) never running out
   (c) extremely tired
   (d) not asleep
   Which vocabulary strategies did you use? _____

   _____

LESSON 3
Word Forms

Word Forms

You have explored using context clues as well as using prefixes and suffixes to figure out the meaning of unknown words. Another strategy to use is to look for the "core" of a word to determine its meaning. Once you have found that core—that "word within a word"—decoding the whole word becomes easier.

For example, the word *establishment* contains the core word *establish* (a verb meaning "to set up, to found"). Once you know the basic meaning of *establish*, you can reason that the *-ment* ending turns the core word into a noun meaning "something set up or founded." In fact, you can apply your knowledge of any core word to work out the meanings of all the other forms (or parts of speech) it might take.

Here are some examples of different formations a core word can take.

Adjective	Noun	Verb	Adverb
decisive	decision	decide	decisively
democratic	democracy	democratize	democratically
necessary	necessity	necessitate	necessarily

Word Forms in Action

Read the following passage.

> The Caribbean is the American Mediterranean in a <u>strategic</u> as well as a <u>climatic</u> sense . . . . The superb arc of islands [the West Indies] has an amazing <u>fertility</u>; the extension of sugar culture around 1650 made even the smallest of them <u>immensely</u> valuable, and the slaves imported from Africa thrived beyond all <u>expectation</u>.
>
> From Morison et al., *The Growth of the American Republic,* p. 48.

The underlined words in the paragraph above may seem difficult. Attacking the words logically makes them much more manageable. For example, the first two words—*strategic* and *climatic*—both end in *-ic*, which is typical of many adjectives. What core words do these two adjectives contain? *Strategy* (meaning "a large-scale plan") is the core word in the first case. *Climate* (meaning "usual or average weather conditions") is the core word in the second. *Strategic*, therefore, means "having to do with strategy," and *climatic* means "having to do with climate."

Word Forms *(continued)*

What word within a word does *fertility* contain? The answer is *fertile* ("rich in resources, fruitful"). The *-ity* ending (which turns adjectives into nouns) gives this word the meaning "the condition or state of being fertile."

How about *immensely*? The word within a word here is the adjective *immense,* which means "enormous, huge." The *-ly* ending usually turns adjectives into adverbs, as is the case here. The meaning of *immensely,* therefore, is "to an enormous extent."

Finally, the word *expectation* contains the core word *expect* (a verb meaning "to look for, to anticipate"). The suffix *-tion,* which turns verbs into nouns, gives this word the meaning "the state of being expected."

Application Read the passage below, then answer the questions that follow. Remember to look for the "words within words" as you analyze each underlined item.

> Despite this <u>tendency</u> to <u>territorial</u> disputes, Indians did not . . . have "ancient" or "traditional" enemies. Each group surely had its allies and [foes], but such relationships were neither permanent nor <u>necessarily</u> long-lived. <u>Alliances</u> changed . . . both before and after European contact. Probably far more frequently than they fought with each other, different peoples learned from each other. Absorbing new influences . . . did not signal the decay or <u>diminution</u> of any culture.
>
> From Milner et al., *The Oxford History of the American West,* pp. 15–16.

1. The word *tendency* means
   (a) a trend or inclination
   (b) being present, attending
   (c) boredom, tediousness
   (d) connecting tissue between bones
   The core word in *tendency* is _____. (Hint: It is a one-syllable verb meaning "to lean, to be directed in a certain way.")

2. The word *territorial* means
   (a) very frightening
   (b) a special breed of dog
   (c) third in a series
   (d) relating to land or property
   The "word within a word" in *territorial* is the noun _____.
   This means _____.

3. The ending of *necessarily* indicates that this word is
   (a) an adverb
   (b) an adjective
   (c) a verb
   (d) a noun
   The core word in *necessarily* is _____ , which means
   _____ .

4. *Alliances* means
   (a) having a certain geographic location
   (b) joining of groups for a common purpose
   (c) deception, lying
   (d) foreigners entering the land
   The two-syllable core word in *alliances* is _____ , which
   means _____ . This word form
   (or part of speech) is a/an _____ .

5. The word *diminution* means
   (a) very low intelligence
   (b) lessening, fading
   (c) faulty weapon
   (d) two nations joining together
   Diminution is a noun of four syllables; the three-syllable verb form of
   this word is _____ .

PART 2
Prereading

LESSON 4
Previewing

When you sit down to read an e-mail from a friend or a magazine article about a sports star, you probably don't go through any complicated procedure. You just read it, enjoy it, then go on your way. When you need to read in order to gather and retain information (for school, let's say), the reading process requires a little more work.

The Reading Process

Good reading actually involves these three stages:

1. Prereading (before reading)
2. Reading
3. Postreading (after reading)

In the lessons that follow, we will take a closer look at each of these stages of reading and what they can mean to you. Let's start with prereading.

Prereading Steps

Prereading (just as the *pre-* prefix implies) is what you do before you read. Prereading involves four steps. These steps are sometimes called the "4 Ps."

Prereading

1. Preview
2. Predict
3. Prior knowledge
4. Purpose

You can organize these steps in a 4-P chart like the one below. Eventually, you will not need a chart. For now, you can use the 4-P chart to remember and practice the prereading steps.

4-P Chart

1. Preview	2. Predict	3. Prior Knowledge	4. Purpose

Previewing *(continued)*

The Importance of Previewing

When you go to the movies, you probably arrive in time to see the previews of coming attractions. What are these previews for? They are designed to spark your interest in new movies. A preview tells you what an upcoming movie is about—the main characters, key events in the plot, and perhaps a problem that needs solving.

In the same way, a first look or preview of something you are about to read can give you important clues about what that reading contains. Previewing helps you get the most important information from your reading, and it helps you remember that information longer.

Previewing

To preview a new chapter in your history book or a long article in a news magazine, what do you do first?

1. **Start with the title.** The title usually tells you the main idea of the entire chapter or article.

2. **Scan** the chapter or article, looking for any highlighted text that is meant to stand out. Watch for headings and subheadings. Be alert for boldfaced or italicized words within paragraphs. Pay attention to bulleted or numbered lists and what they seem to be about.

3. **Look at the graphics** in your reading selection. Graphics are photos, drawings, maps, charts, graphs, time lines—any text elements that are not just words.

4. **Skim** the chapter or article. When you skim, you do not read word for word. You should read the first and last paragraphs in each major section of the text. If you are working with a shorter passage, read the first and last lines in each paragraph.

Previewing *(continued)*

Application   Use your prereading skills to preview the following selection from a United States history text. Do *not* read the entire article—just preview it! Fill in the Preview column of the 4-P chart that follows the article.

The Nation Keeps Growing (1793–1874)

Time Line

Events Elsewhere	Date	Events in America
	1793	Whitney invented cotton gin
	1803	Louisiana Purchase
	1807	Fulton used steam to power *Clermont*
	1812–14	War of 1812
Napoleon defeated at Waterloo	1815	
	1818	National Road
Mexico gained freedom from Spain	1821	
	1822	Austin guided Americans into Texas
	1825	Erie Canal completed
	1828	Andrew Jackson elected president
	1830	Cooper developed steam locomotive
Slavery abolished in Britain	1833	
	1836	Texas free from Mexico; Battle of Alamo; Whitman's mission in Oregon
	1840	McKay's clipper ship
	1844	Morse developed telegraph
	1845	Howe invented sewing machine; Texas became a state
	1846	Mexican War began; U.S. acquired Oregon Country
	1848	End of Mexican War; gold discovered in California
	1849	California gold rush
	1850	California became a state
	1853	Gadsden Purchase
	1860	Pony Express began

Territorial Expansion

At the dawn of the nineteenth century, the United States had grown from thirteen colonies into a nation that was beginning to claim international recognition. After the Louisiana Purchase, effected by President Thomas Jefferson, the nation's western border now extended far beyond the Mississippi River, and its northern and western borders now included a major portion of the Missouri River. The country had doubled its territory in a relatively brief time.

Achievements in Transportation and Communication

In order for a nation to remain united and effective, there must be an easy and efficient way for people, goods, and ideas to move from one part of the country to another. Five important technological developments helped bring most parts of the new nation closer together by speeding transportation and improving communication. These involved roads, canals, steamships, railroads, and telegraph lines.

Early **roads** were narrow, potholed, and muddy when it rained. Therefore, just before the beginning of the War of 1812, the government started building the **National Road.** When it was finally finished, it ran from western Maryland to central Illinois—the finest road in America at the time. People traveling on this road bought supplies in the towns and villages located along the way. Many merchants benefited from this business, and the resulting prosperity helped many of the towns to grow.

For transportation by water, a major innovation was the building of **canals.** Canals were dug to connect bodies of water where no natural waterways existed. Horses or mules walking on land pulled canal boats or barges through the water. Such travel was cheap but slow. The governor of New York, De Witt Clinton, soon realized how valuable this cheap transportation could be. He arranged for the building of the **Erie Canal,** which connected the New York cities of Albany and Buffalo. When the 363-mile-long canal was finished in 1825, it was possible to go by boat from New York City to the Great Lakes in about ten days.

Steamship

Until 1807, the only way to move a boat upriver or against the current was by using oars, poles, or towropes powered by men or mules. Eventually, an American named Robert Fulton decided that a steam engine could be used to power a ship. Many people thought that Fulton was wrong; his first **steamship,** the *Clermont,* was called "Fulton's Folly" by skeptics. Then, one day in 1807, the *Clermont's* huge paddle wheel began to turn, driving the ship up the Hudson River. On that historic voyage, Fulton's ship traveled 300 miles in just over 60 hours. The age of steam transportation had begun.

Adapted from *Short Lessons in U.S. History,* by E. Richard Churchill and Linda R. Churchill. © 1999 by J. Weston Walch, Publisher.

Previewing *(continued)*

Ask yourself these questions to help you fill in the Preview column of the 4-P chart. Some information has been filled in to get you started.

1. What does the chapter title tell you about the main idea of this reading selection?
2. What concepts are expressed in the headings and subheadings?
3. What key words are highlighted in the text?
4. When you skimmed the first and last paragraphs, and the first and last sentences in each paragraph, what ideas seemed to be most important?
5. What graphic elements are included? What do these graphics emphasize?

4-P Chart

1. Preview	2. Predict	3. Prior Knowledge	4. Purpose
1. Territorial expansion			
2.			
3. Key words: roads—National Road canals—Erie Canal			
4. Key ideas: U.S. doubled territory— 19th century Importance of easy transport and communication			
5.			

LESSON 5
Predicting

Predicting

Have you ever seen television commercials or magazine ads promoting the services of people who claim to be able to "see" the future? These services may promise to tell you what will happen later in your life. These people are claiming to predict what will happen to you at some future date.

Prediction may not work very well in fortune-telling, but it is a powerful tool in reading. In order to get the maximum benefit from what you read, you should make predicting a regular strategy in your reading process.

Application

Using the information you gathered during the previewing stage (see Lesson 4), you can now predict what you think will happen in the reading on page 17. Here are some key questions to help you predict what the reading is all about. Use these questions to help you fill in the Predict column of the 4-P chart.

1. Based on your preview, what do you think this reading passage focuses on?
2. Which topic (or topics) seems to be covered in the most depth in this reading?
3. What do you think you will learn from your reading?
4. What do you think the main idea or thesis of this reading might be?

4-P Chart

1. Preview	2. Predict	3. Prior Knowledge	4. Purpose
	1. focuses on transportation development. 2. 3. will tell what developments were . . . 4.		

LESSON 6
Prior Knowledge

What happens when you begin to read something new? Do you just read the words and let them flow into your mind? Is your brain like an empty container, which this new reading material will simply fill up?

The answer is "no." Reading is never a completely passive activity. Whenever you read, you bring your own life experience to the reading. In many cases, you will already know something about the subject covered in the reading selection. This information you already possess is called your **prior knowledge.**

When you read, you make connections between the information in the text and the prior knowledge in your head. Successful readers are active readers, always drawing from their storehouse of prior knowledge, relating it to what they're reading, and adding any new information to that store.

Application   You have already previewed the reading on page 17, and you have made some predictions about it. Now, make some connections between what you think the reading is about and what you already know about this subject— your prior knowledge.

Now do some brainstorming. Look back at the 4-P columns you have filled in for Lessons 4 and 5. What words or ideas come to mind when you think about this topic or these topics? Write as many related words, facts, and thoughts as possible in the Prior Knowledge column below.

4-P Chart

1. Preview	2. Predict	3. Prior Knowledge	4. Purpose

ESSON 7
Purpose

The Reader's Purpose

Why do people read? There are many reasons. Some people love reading for its own sake. They read for enjoyment.

Others read to gather information. They read a daily newspaper, perhaps subscribe to a weekly newsmagazine, and may on occasion tackle a nonfiction book—a political biography, for example. They are reading to be well informed.

Still others read only when it is required—by a classroom teacher, or by a supervisor on the job to develop special workplace skills. These people choose to devote time to reading only when there is a clear educational purpose or specific reward (perhaps better grades or higher pay). They read to learn.

Application

Before you start to read, ask yourself what your purpose is. Your answer will help you determine which reading strategies to use. For the article you've been working with on page 17, your purpose has been mainly to practice the prereading steps. Imagine now that you have been assigned the article for social studies class. In the 4-P chart below, fill in what your purpose for reading would be—what do you want to gain by reading?

4-P Chart

1. Preview	2. Predict	3. Prior Knowledge	4. Purpose

Purpose *(continued)*

The Writer's Purpose

Why do people write? Again, there are many reasons. Some authors write for the sheer enjoyment of it. They write out of love for the craft, out of a desire to tell good stories and give pleasure to others. They write primarily to entertain.

Others write to let the public know about the world around them. They may become news writers, art critics, or authors of history and biography. They write to inform. Other writers want to share some special knowledge with a very particular audience. They write how-to books, algebra texts, or medical papers. They are writing to teach.

Author Bias

In an earlier lesson, you learned that readers bring their personal experience, or prior knowledge, to a piece of reading. In the same way, every author brings his or her own personal experience to a piece of writing. This influences what the author chooses to write about and how he or she writes it. In fact, authors can sometimes feel so strongly about a subject that their emotions or judgments color their writing. They may leave out facts that contradict their personal opinions, or they may include information that is not necessarily proved to be true. Writing that is slanted toward one viewpoint at the expense of another is biased writing. It is important to consider the writer's viewpoint, or author bias, every time you read.

Now read the entire passage on page 17. When you have finished, answer the following questions.

1. Did your prereading activities prepare you for what you actually learned when you read the whole passage? Why or why not?

2. What was the author's purpose in writing the passage? Why do you think so?

PART 3
Reading Strategies

LESSON 8
Introduction to Reading Strategies

Now that you have learned and practiced the four key prereading steps, you can turn your attention to the second stage in the overall reading process: the reading itself. How do you get the maximum benefit from the reading stage?

Graphic Organizers

One way successful readers learn and retain information is by using graphic organizers. Despite the fancy name, graphic organizers are really just simple charts that you can make and use yourself. While reading, you fill in your graphic organizer. It helps you arrange your thoughts, note key concepts and terms from the reading, and clarify the main ideas.

Since writing something helps to reinforce it, the act of filling in a graphic organizer makes new material easier for your brain to recall. In addition, the visual arrangement of the words and concepts in a graphic organizer gives your brain a "picture" of the information you need to remember.

Kinds of Graphic Organizers

Here are some of the most effective graphic organizers used by readers.

KWL—The KWL organizer consists of three sections: (1) **K** = what I already know about a particular subject; (2) **W** = what I want to know about the subject; and (3) **L** = what I learned about the subject from the reading.

SQ3R—This organizer consists of five sections, each representing a step in the reading process: (1) **S** = survey; (2) **Q** = question; (3) the first **R** = read; (4) the second **R** = recall; (5) the third **R** = reflect.

Semantic Web—This type of graphic organizer can take many different forms. It usually consists of a central circle (or other shape) representing a main idea or main character in the reading. Supporting ideas and details then branch out from the center, forming a more or less complex web.

Outline—Outlining is the most linear of the graphic organizers. An outline helps the reader arrange material in a methodical, step-by-step manner. Outlines often reflect the skeleton of a reading selection.

Structured Notes—This type of organizer can take a variety of forms. The goal is to help readers arrange their notes in a systematic, logical manner based on the structure of the reading selection.

LESSON 9
KWL

KWL

As you learned in Lesson 8, the letters in KWL stand for

K = what I already **know** (about the topic)

W = what I **want** to know (about the topic)

L = what I **learned** from the reading

The K and W steps involve the prereading process. **K** asks for the reader's prior knowledge (what I already know), and **W** seeks a purpose for reading (what I want to learn). This is the sort of information you would find in a 4-P chart. The **L** step is what happens after reading (the postreading process), when the reader asks, "What did I learn from this?"

A typical KWL organizer looks like the one below.

K	W	L
Prior **know**ledge—some facts about this topic that I have already learned; concepts I already **know**	What else I **want** to know about this topic; questions I have that give me a purpose for reading	What I **learned** from this reading; new facts, ideas, or viewpoints that I had not considered before

KWL in Action

The following passage is about French Renaissance castles. The KWL chart that follows it has been filled in for you. Study the **K** and **W** sections of the organizer first; then read the passage. Finally, look at the **L** section of the organizer to see what the reader learned. Is there anything you might add?

During the French Renaissance, the royalty and noble families of France were greatly influenced by the impressive artistic achievements of their Italian neighbors. Hoping to capture some of the style and elegance of artists like Da Vinci and Michelangelo, the French aristocracy either built magnificent new chateaux (castles) or added major additions and ornaments to their existing medieval homes.

The most splendid chateaux—including Chambord, Chenonceaux, Azay-le-Rideau, and Usse (the inspiration for the Sleeping Beauty legend) — were built between the mid-1400s and the late 1500s. Scores of such chateaux are still to be found (and visited) in the Loire River valley, southwest of Paris. This is where the kings of France hunted, entertained, plotted, and ruled during most of the Renaissance. These days of glory ended when Henri IV moved his court back to Paris at the close of the sixteenth century.

K What I KNOW	W What I WANT to Know	L What I LEARNED
Renaissance = came after the Middle Ages France's capital is Paris. Castles = where wealthy and powerful lived; offered protection from enemies	When did this happen? Where were these castles built? Do they still exist?	mid 1400s–end of 1500s Loire valley = SW of Paris Many exist; can be visited. One chateau inspired Sleeping Beauty story. This (not Paris) was where kings actually ruled for many years.

Application Look at following passage about the Ming Dynasty. What do you already know about the subject? Jot down what you know in the space under the **K** in the graphic organizer that follows the reading. In the space under the **W,** write what else you want to know about this subject. Now read the passage.

KWL (continued)

The last native Chinese dynasty in history was the Ming, succeeding the Mongols and ruling a vast empire from 1368 to 1644. Ming rule began under a rebel leader named Zhu. The dynasty's first emperor, he was given the name Hongwu. As supreme head of state with absolute power, Hongwu ordered the killing of thousands of government officials and provincial leaders who resisted his rise to power. He created a strong central government, which at first unified the huge and diverse empire.

Most citizens lived and worked on small farms throughout the Chinese countryside, receiving little or no education, while the educated elite—including a large class of civil servants—lived in large cities like Nanjing (the new capital), Beijing, and Guangzhou. The population, now better fed than in earlier centuries, grew from 60 million at the dawn of this dynasty to about 150 million at its close.

The Ming had an enormous impact on Chinese art and culture. They were best known for their beautiful porcelains and ceramics (which were often exported), works of literature, and silk and cotton weaving. The Ming dynasty also sponsored many daring sea explorations, built the Great Wall, laid out new roads, and constructed the Great Canal linking Beijing with the Yangtze and Huang He rivers.

Eventually, Ming authority in the capital began to weaken as Mongol invaders on the northern border, Japanese pirates on the south coast, and overtaxed peasants within the empire itself made repeated attacks that the centralized government could not defend itself against. Defeated by a foreign tribe in Manchuria in 1619, Ming rule began to unravel. The northern invaders made further encroachments into Chinese territory until they founded the Qing dynasty, which officially began in 1644.

What did you learn from this reading? Write your answers in the space under the **L** in the KWL chart below.

K What I KNOW	W What I WANT to Know	L What I LEARNED

QUIZ

Complete the following statements, which are based on the reading about the Ming dynasty.

1. The word *encroachment* in the last sentence of the passage means
   (a) crouching down, lying low to the ground
   (b) an invasion of harmful insects
   (c) villages or towns surrounded by tall fencing
   (d) trespassing or intruding

2. The Ming dynasty was well known for
   (a) fine regional cuisine
   (b) porcelain and ceramic exports
   (c) daring temple architecture
   (d) a strong educational system for all citizens

3. The population probably received better nutrition during the Ming dynasty because
   (a) there were fewer people to share the food supply
   (b) mothers attended school to learn how to prepare healthier meals
   (c) climate changes lengthened the growing season
   (d) imported items and better transportation gave people more access to good food

4. The Ming dynasty failed largely because of
   (a) foreign invasions and rebellions from the large class of civil servants
   (b) pirate invasions and the fall of the Great Wall
   (c) foreign invasions in the north and the south, as well as peasant rebellions
   (d) lack of money due to too many exports and foreign wars

5. The strong central government of the Ming dynasty
   (a) also proved to be its downfall in the long run
   (b) empowered the peasant classes through its system of irrigation canals
   (c) provided the best military defense against foreign invaders
   (d) served as a model for future governments, including that of the United States

LESSON 10
SQ3R

SQ3R

In an earlier lesson, you learned that another powerful graphic organizer to use when you read is called SQ3R. Although the three Rs in this organizer have meant different things to different people over the years, an effective definition in use today is

S = Survey; Q = Question; R = Read; R = Recall; R = Reflect

Like the KWL organizer, the SQ3R includes some of the prereading steps that you would follow to complete a 4-P chart. For example, the **S** (survey) and **Q** (question) steps fall into the prereading category. SQ3R also involves reading (covered in the first **R**) and postreading (covered in the second and third **R**s).

Here is what a typical SQ3R organizer looks like.

S	Q	R	R	R
Preview the reading; **survey** text and art. Note key items.	Make predictions. Ask **questions.** Decide your purpose for reading.	**Read** the selection with care; make notes as you read.	Take time to review the reading; on paper, **recall** the most important points.	Think about what you've learned; **reflect** on what this means.

SQ3R in Action

The following reading passage is about economic inflation. The SQ3R chart that follows the passage has been filled in to show you how someone might use this chart while reading. Study the **S** and **Q** sections of the organizer first. Then read the passage. Next, look at the first **R** section to see what was noted during reading. Finally, look at the last two **R** sections to see what the reader learned. Is there anything you might add?

One of the greatest threats to a market economy is **inflation.** Simply put, inflation results in the diminished purchasing power of money. This in turn leads to higher prices. Naturally, higher prices mean that many people can no longer afford to buy the items they want or need. Workers therefore have two choices: to seek higher rates of pay from their employers, or to lower their own **standard of living.** Otherwise, they must borrow money or deplete their personal savings to maintain their current levels of spending.

Most workers first opt to demand higher wages in order to keep up with the inflation rate. As a result of granting pay increases, however, employers then raise the prices of their goods and services. Other consumers have to pay more for the higher-priced items, which means that they in turn need to seek higher pay to maintain their current standard of living. This continuing cycle of increasing prices and wages is called an **inflationary spiral.**

Adapted from *Understanding Our Economy,* by E. Richard Churchill and Linda R. Churchill. © 1998 by J. Weston Walch, Publisher.

S Survey	Q Question	R Read	R Recall	R Reflect
<u>Key terms:</u> *inflation,* *standard of* *living,* *inflationary* *spiral* Inflation = threat to economy	What is inflation? <u>Prior knowledge</u>: *standard of living* = way we usually live, spend money	Inflation = less buying power Results in workers seeking more $$ Leads to higher prices (cycle/spiral)	Review definitions of 3 boldfaced terms. Summarize all main points.	People with low or fixed incomes could be at larger disadvantage during inflation—can't raise their pay. Risk of more citizens getting into debt.

Application   The following passage is about the treatment of Japanese Americans during World War II. Using the SQ3R graphic organizer that follows the passage, first survey the reading. Make notes of the most important terms and concepts in the section under the **S.** Then connect these with your prior knowledge and question what else you want to know. Note this in the **Q** section of the chart. Finally, read the passage, jotting down new information in the section under the first **R.**

Two months after a Japanese air bombardment devastated the United States naval fleet at Pearl Harbor, President Franklin Roosevelt signed Executive Order 9066. Dated February 19, 1942, this law ordered the removal of all Americans of Japanese ancestry from their homes. In all, more than 110,000 Japanese Americans—most of whom lived in Hawaii or on the West Coast—were affected.

Virtually none of these citizens was considered a threat to national security by U.S. intelligence agencies. Nevertheless, political leaders from both major parties were swayed by anti-Japanese prejudice on the part of the public. Most members of Congress therefore supported the president's action.

Japanese-American citizens of all ages were rounded up by American military personnel and taken to any one of sixteen temporary "assembly centers," which had been quickly erected in isolated spots, like fairgrounds and racetracks, far from the Pacific coast. Of the sixteen camps, thirteen were in California; the other three were in Washington, Oregon, and Arizona. Most "detainees" were forced to stay in these assembly centers for four or five months, while more permanent—and more isolated—internment camps were built. Eventually, ten such camps were built, most of them in lonely desert areas with harsh climates. There many of the prisoners remained—fed and housed, but deprived of most of the rights supposedly granted to all U.S. citizens—for the duration of the war. In the words of one detainee, "I could never figure out what they thought we were going to do. Born and raised in a typical American home. Middle-income people. Then to have this happen, you wonder why. What'd I do?"

What did you learn from this reading? Try to recall the main points. Write them in the section under the second **R.** Next, take some time to reflect. What does this reading mean to you? What important points is this author trying to make? Note this in the section under the third **R.**

S Survey	Q Question	R Read	R Recall	R Reflect

QUIZ

Complete the following statements, which are based on the reading about the internment of Japanese Americans.

1. The word *devastated* in the first sentence means
   (a) covered a very large area
   (b) devalued, lowered the price of
   (c) completely destroyed
   (d) changed it from a state to another form of government

2. In the context of the third paragraph, the word *internment* means
   (a) confinement or imprisonment
   (b) training in a medical setting like a hospital
   (c) a place for an apprentice to learn a new skill or job
   (d) a place for reflective thinking and meditation

3. Executive Order 9066 ordered the removal of
   (a) all people visiting the United States from Japan
   (b) all Japanese Americans living on the West Coast
   (c) all Japanese citizens with American ancestry
   (d) all Americans with Japanese ancestry

4. Political leaders probably allowed themselves to be swayed by anti-Japanese feelings because they
   (a) had access to special information about Japanese-American terrorists
   (b) were worried that harm would come to American citizens from the West Coast
   (c) did not want to displease the people who elected them
   (d) wanted to prevent Japanese Americans from moving to Washington, DC

5. Residents of the internment camps were deprived of many rights of citizenship
   (a) including liberty, since they were not free to come and go as they pleased
   (b) including access to shelter and food
   (c) because they had voluntarily given up these rights to prove their loyalty
   (d) because they posed a serious threat to American security

LESSON 11
Semantic Web

Semantic Web   Semantic webs can take many different forms. These graphic organizers generally resemble a spider's web. They contain a central circle (or other shape) representing a major idea or a major character in a reading selection. Supporting ideas and details fan or branch out from the central shape, forming the rest of the web. Completing a semantic web can help you sort out main ideas versus details. It can also help you clarify a cause versus its effects.

A typical semantic web might look something like this.

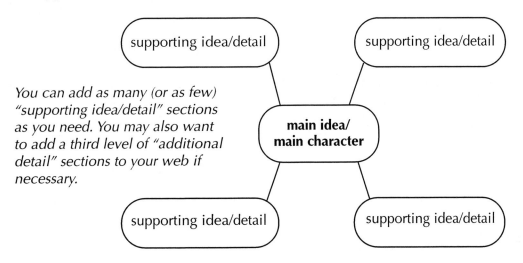

You can add as many (or as few) "supporting idea/detail" sections as you need. You may also want to add a third level of "additional detail" sections to your web if necessary.

Semantic Web in Action   The reading passage that follows is about an archeological site in Mexico. The semantic web that follows it has been filled in to show you how someone might use this organizer while reading. Read the passage. Then study the semantic web. Is there anything you might change?

Semantic Web *(continued)*

For centuries, the ancient Mexican ruins of Palenque were forgotten deep in the Yucatán, smothered by dense rain forests. An occasional explorer had glimpsed and recorded some of Palenque's marvels, but the reports went largely unnoticed. Those who did pay any heed to this Maya civilization noted a resemblance to ancient Egyptian culture. Some pyramids, statues, and relief carvings found at Palenque did resemble their Egyptian counterparts. Eighteenth-century historians therefore surmised that, at some much earlier point, there had been a colony of Egyptians in Mesoamerica.

Then, in 1840, explorers Stephens and Catherwood made the hazardous trip through the jungle to Palenque. This time, the team took greater care in examining the vine-covered ruins. They discovered a 300-foot-long, stucco-decorated palace complex with a system of courtyards and detailed, grotesque carvings of human figures. They also discovered temples built upon large pyramids, stone tablets carved with unique hieroglyphic writing, and many other remains of a large, sophisticated ancient city. The explorers were convinced that, despite a slight resemblance to Egyptian art, Palenque bore no real traces of Egyptian culture whatsoever: "It is the spectacle of a people . . . originating and growing up here, without models or masters, having a distinct, separate, indigenous existence . . . like the plants and fruits of the soil. . . ." This began a new perception of the Maya as a culture in their own right.

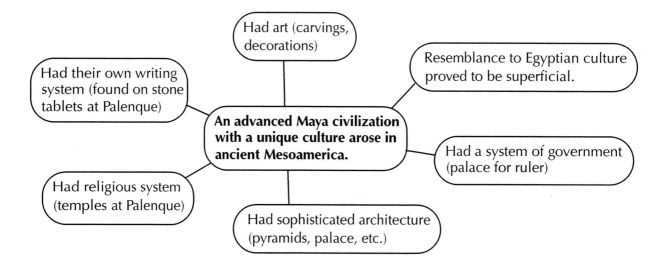

Application The following passage is about African Americans during the Civil War. Read the selection carefully. Then fill in the semantic web at the bottom of the page to help you record the main idea and details in the reading.

Semantic Web *(continued)*

The Fugitive Slave Act required anyone who captured an escaped slave to return the unfortunate man, woman, or child to the South. During the Civil War, however, Union generals arranged to keep runaways as "contraband of war." This meant that they were enemy property and did not need to be returned. All in all, about 200,000 escaped slaves became paid laborers for the Union cause during the war. They dug trenches, built forts, and loaded supply wagons.

As the war dragged on, many of these laborers became volunteer soldiers, although the U.S. government did not recognize them officially until July 1862. Then Congress passed a law allowing African Americans to be paid for fighting for the Union army. Just a few months later, a black regiment from Kansas was engaged in a battle in Missouri—the first time African Americans had officially fought on American soil.

During the course of the war, many black regiments fought heroically for the North. In July 1863, for example, the Fifty-fourth Massachusetts Regiment took the lead in a major attack on Fort Wagner in South Carolina. Forty-two percent of the regiment were killed or wounded in this one battle; their heroism inspired many other African Americans to enlist.

By the end of the war, black soldiers had undoubtedly helped the Union win the Civil War. The numbers are impressive: 186,000 African Americans served in the Union army; about 29,000 served in the navy. Of these men, a total of 38,000 died in the war. African Americans fought in at least 39 major battles and 400 smaller engagements, from Bull Run to Appomattox. In addition, countless others participated behind the lines, serving as spies, scouts, nurses, and teachers. The contribution of African Americans to the Union's victory cannot be underestimated.

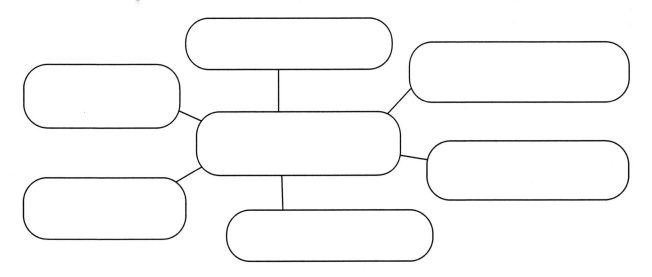

QUIZ

Complete the following statements, which are based on the reading about African Americans during the Civil War.

1. The word *fugitive* means
   (a) useless or futile
   (b) running away
   (c) forgetful, neglectful
   (d) taking refuge

2. A *regiment* is a
   (a) military unit of soldiers
   (b) political system
   (c) regulated system of diet and exercise
   (d) particular geographic location

3. The Union army was interested in keeping escaped slaves as "contraband" mostly because
   (a) they were eager for the reward money from the South
   (b) they needed the labor that the escaped slaves could provide
   (c) it was too difficult to return them to their rightful owners during the war
   (d) the Union generals were staging a formal protest of the Fugitive Slave Act

4. Including black soldiers in the Union army and Union navy, the total number of African Americans who served officially during the Civil War was
   (a) 38,000
   (b) 86,000
   (c) 186,000
   (d) 215,000

5. Many African Americans were actually willing to serve as unpaid volunteers in the early years of the war; this was probably because
   (a) they did not need the money
   (b) the Fugitive Slave Act allowed them to do so
   (c) they had been well trained for battle before enlisting
   (d) they hoped it would help them escape slavery

LESSON 12
Outline

Outline An outline is one of the most step by step, or sequential, of graphic organizers. An outline helps readers—and writers—arrange material in a methodical manner.

Making an Outline Traditionally, the main ideas are labeled with Roman numerals. Major supporting information is labeled with capital letters. The next level of information is labeled with Arabic numerals, and the level below that, with lowercase letters. A typical outline might look something like this.

Major Subject or Topic (This could be the title of the reading.)

I. Main idea
   A. Detail
      1. supporting information (if applicable)
      2. next supporting information (if applicable)
         a. more information about 2
   B. Second detail
   C. Third detail (if applicable)

II. Next main idea
   A. Detail
   B. Second detail
   C. Third detail (if applicable)

III. Next main idea (if applicable)

Outline in Action The following reading passage is about the Articles of Confederation. The outline that follows the reading has been completed to show you how someone might use this organizer while reading. Read the passage yourself; then study the outline. Is there anything you might change?

The Articles of Confederation were voted into life by Congress in March 1781 while the Revolutionary War still raged. The change in government outlined in the Articles simply formalized what had been taking place since 1775, when war first broke out. The Congress of the new Confederation, like the earlier Continental Congress, consisted of members representing each of the thirteen states in the new nation. Each state was allotted between two and seven members, and each member was limited to three years in office out of any six. Each state got one vote.

Some changes in governmental structure included a requirement that nine out of thirteen states (in other words, a clear majority) agree by vote whenever a major congressional decision had to be made. Such possibilities included going to war, raising armed forces, making treaties with other nations, or taking on debt. A final possibility was appointing a new commander-in-chief, or president.

Another change included giving Congress the power to appoint five special governmental departments: foreign affairs, war, the admiralty, finance, and the post office.

Articles of Confederation

I. Similarities to previous government

    A. members represented all 13 states

    B. each state got 2–7 members

        1. 3-year terms every 6 years

    C. 1 vote per state

II. Differences from previous government

    A. 9 out of 13 states had to agree by vote for key items

        1. war

        2. raising army

        3. treaties

        4. debt

        5. choosing president

    B. Congress got 5 new departments

        1. foreign affairs

        2. war

        3. admiralty

        4. finance

        5. post office

Outline *(continued)*

Application   The following passage is about the Hawaiian Islands. Read the selection carefully. Then fill in the outline that follows the selection to help you record the main points of the reading. You will probably want to change the outline by adding or removing lines.

> The Hawaiian Islands were first settled well over a millennium ago by Polynesians from other islands in the South Pacific. After this original ancient settlement, there were no further known foreign visitors to the Hawaiian island group until the arrival of Captain James Cook in 1778. Thus, for many centuries a unique Hawaiian culture developed from its Polynesian roots, free from any outside influences.
>
> This tropical island chain was formed through a series of volcanic eruptions that occurred hundreds of thousands of years ago. Volcanoes under the ocean floor sent molten lava upward through the water. The lava broke the water's surface, then settled and cooled, forming the beautiful islands that we know today.
>
> Spanning an area that covers more than one thousand miles, the Hawaiian Islands remain geographically isolated. The Aleutians far to the north, and the Marquesas Islands far to the south, are their nearest neighbors—yet both island chains are at least two thousand miles away.

I. _____

   A. _____

       1. _____

       2. _____

       3. _____

   B. _____

       1. _____

       2. _____

       3. _____

II. _____

   A. _____

   B. _____

   C. _____

QUIZ

Complete the following statements, which are based on the reading about the Hawaiian Islands.

1. The word *millennium* means
   - (a) one hundred years
   - (b) one thousand years
   - (c) one million years
   - (d) before recorded history

2. The word *molten* in this passage means
   - (a) tunneling through the water
   - (b) shedding some of its mass as it moves
   - (c) melted due to heat
   - (d) similar to mold

3. The original settlers of the Hawaiian islands came from
   - (a) the Aleutians
   - (b) the Marquesas
   - (c) Captain James Cook's expedition
   - (d) Polynesian islands in the South Pacific

4. The Hawaiian Islands were undisturbed by foreign settlers for many years because
   - (a) the Polynesians kept them out
   - (b) the volcanoes were too threatening
   - (c) they are too rocky for easy landing by ship
   - (d) they are physically very distant

5. The Hawaiian culture probably
   - (a) retained some Polynesian features
   - (b) became very English after Cook's arrival
   - (c) was highly influenced by the people of the Aleutians
   - (d) was highly influenced by the people of the Marquesas

LESSON 13
Structured Notes

Structured Notes

You may have already learned something about taking notes. This may have involved jotting down important facts while researching a term paper. Maybe you wrote down key terms and ideas during a class discussion. However, most of us take notes in a casual way without organizing our thoughts or arranging our notes. Structured notes help readers do just that.

In structured notetaking, your paper is divided into important categories and transformed into a graphic organizer. A structured note page might look like one of the following:

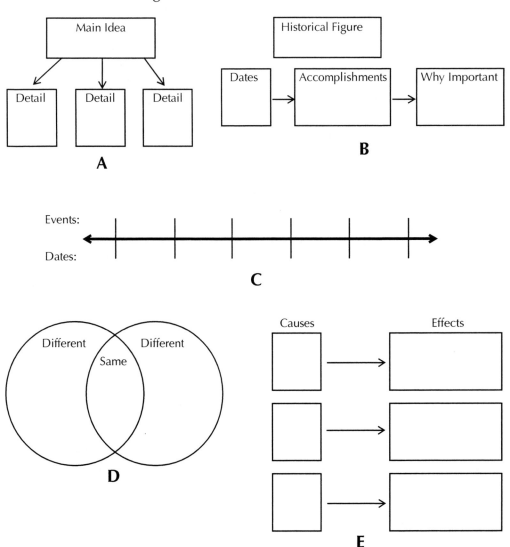

Structured Notes (continued)

The exact wording for the headings on your paper will vary according to your reading purpose and the nature of the reading selection itself. If you follow the prereading steps outlined in Lessons 4–7, you will probably have a good idea about which headings will work best.

Structured Notes in Action

Read the passage below. Then look at the structured notes that follow to see how one reader kept track of the material.

In the early 600s, at the time when Muhammad first began preaching, Arabia was largely populated by nomadic tribal peoples known as Bedouins. These wandering groups traveled with herds of sheep and goats over the Arabian peninsula, seeking grazing lands among the many areas of desert. The rest of the Arabian population was concentrated in towns and settlements along the Red Sea or in the southern valleys. The most notable of these settlements were in the Hejaz region in the northwest, Mecca, Medina, and Yemen.

There was no centralized government to speak of in Arabia at this time. Tribal laws and loyalties ruled the lives of most people. The family unit was extremely close-knit and proud, and the Arab's life was largely occupied with family obligations and certain religious observances.

Although Muhammad would soon transform their religious life, Arabs of this era still practiced Zoroastrianism, which emphasized the individual's free will to choose between good and evil in life. All Arabs, regardless of tribe, reserved three months each year to devote to religious ceremonies. During that period, they ceased all fighting and concentrated on prayer and pilgrimage to the Kaaba sanctuary in Mecca, the center of their holy world.

Main Idea	Details
Arabian population in early 600s ⟶	Nomadic tribes (Bedouins) —raised sheep, goats A few towns/settlements (Red Sea & valleys in south) —Mecca, Medina, Yemen, Hejaz
Government ⟶	Tribal law; no centralized govt.
Social organization ⟶	Family unit most important
Religion ⟶	Zoroastrianism (good vs. evil) 3 mos./yr. for prayer & peace —pilgrimage to Kaaba (Mecca)

Structured Notes *(continued)*

Application   The following passage is about the early Puritans. Read the selection carefully. Then use the organizer that follows. You may want to change headings or create a completely different graphic organizer. Do what works best for you.

The Puritans who first colonized New England were in fact a small splinter group who had broken away from the powerful Church of England. They were frustrated by the many levels of church officials who dominated their parish priests. They were also deeply disturbed by the extravagance and questionable morals of English society. This small band of farmers, shopkeepers, and manual laborers therefore moved to Leyden, in the Netherlands, in 1609. There they stayed for ten years, worshipping at their own English Congregational Church and living in poverty but in peace.

Around 1619, however, war was threatening in the Netherlands. The Puritans, seeking a different home where they could have complete freedom of religion, decided to try a new life on a very distant shore: America. A group of generous English merchants agreed to fund their voyage, even obtaining a land grant for the Puritans from the Virginia Company.

In the fall of 1620, in the harshest sailing season of the year, this brave and ill-prepared group set sail in the *Mayflower.* They arrived in Cape Cod Bay on November 11, outside the limits of the Virginia Company's lands. Not knowing where their final settlement would be, but aware of their need to work together to survive, these English citizens quickly wrote and signed an agreement stating that the will of the majority would rule them until further notice. This was the Mayflower Compact, which would prove to be a cornerstone of American democracy.

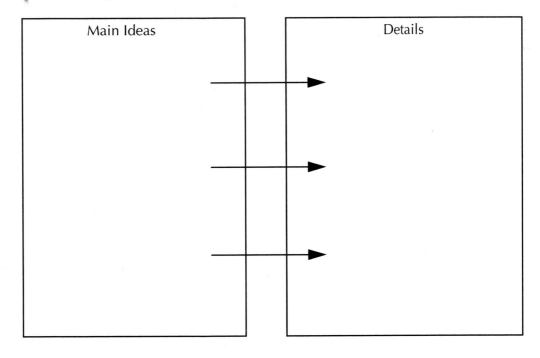

Main Ideas	Details

QUIZ

Complete each of the following statements, which are based on the reading on the previous page about the Puritans.

1. The word *extravagance* means
   (a) going beyond reasonable limits in buying or behavior
   (b) wandering outside, with no home of one's own
   (c) taking things away from others
   (d) getting revenge for a wrong that has been committed

2. To live in *poverty* is to live
   (a) with very little money
   (b) with a great deal of political power
   (c) in small apartment houses
   (d) where the gunpowder for weapons was stored

3. The Puritans chose America for their new home because
   (a) many of them had relatives there
   (b) many New England businesses were offering jobs
   (c) their church in the Netherlands was destroyed in the war
   (d) they wanted to practice their own religion without interference

4. The Puritans were mostly
   (a) of royal or aristocratic birth
   (b) parish priests
   (c) shopkeepers and laborers
   (d) sailors and soldiers

5. The Mayflower Compact was important for two reasons:
   (a) It was written on the *Mayflower,* and it formed a democracy.
   (b) It was written by the Puritans, and it was written in English.
   (c) It was the first Compact ever written, and it formed the Puritans' government.
   (d) It gave the Puritans a form of government, and it helped form American democracy.

 Content-Area Reading Strategies: Social Studies

PART 4
Postreading

LESSON 14
Summarizing and Paraphrasing

After Reading   What do you do after you finish reading? Do you slam your textbook shut and say, "Finally! That's done—now I can check my e-mail"? Or do you practice postreading strategies? It is important to think about what you have learned from your reading. (Think of the L in the KWL chart.) To do this, you need to spend a little time reflecting on what the text is really saying and what conclusions you can draw from it. (Think of the last R in SQ3R.)

One of the most powerful ways to show that you have really understood a reading selection is to retell it briefly yourself. There are two ways to retell the main points of a reading:

- Summarizing—using words that all come directly from the reading
- Paraphrasing—using mostly your own words

Summarizing and Paraphrasing in Action   The reading passage below is about how companies sell stock. It is followed by a summary and a paraphrase that retell the most important points of the reading passage. Read the passage first. Then read the summary and paraphrase. Do they include all the main points?

When a for-profit business needs funding to expand or to otherwise improve its facilities and products, how does it raise the funds? Many companies choose to sell stock, or shares in the business. By selling stock to a number of people, who then become shareholders, the company can receive the capital it needs in order to grow. At this point, the company offering the stock to outside buyers is no longer a private business. It becomes a publicly traded company, which shares all financial risks—as well as the profits—with its shareholders.

There are three types of shares (or securities) that companies often offer to their investors: bonds, preferred stock, and common stock. Each of these securities offers a different level of financial risk, should the company not perform as well as expected, and a different level of potential reward, should the business succeed.

Summarizing and Paraphrasing (*continued*)

Summary

> When a business needs funding, it may choose to sell stock, or shares in the business. The stock buyers become shareholders. Then the business becomes a publicly traded company. It shares the financial risks and profits with the shareholders. There are three types of shares (securities): bonds, preferred stock, and common stock. Each offers a different financial risk and a different level of reward.

Paraphrase

> If a company needs to raise money, it may decide to sell stock. Then people who are not employees of the company own a part of the business. When this happens, the business is not private any more; it is a public corporation. All of the stock owners then have a "piece of the pie," so if the business does well, they make money, too; if the business does poorly, so do they. You can get three kinds of shares: bonds, preferred stock, and common stock. They don't cost the same amount of money to buy, and they don't earn the same amount of profit.

Application The following passage is about Midwestern prairie farmers in the 1800s. Read the selection carefully, using whichever graphic organizer you like to note important information.

> In the middle of the nineteenth century, prairie farmers in the American Midwest were the most common kind of pioneer. The fertile land of this region produced bumper crops on a fairly predictable basis, and the rising prices that could be asked for wheat in eastern markets like New York made farming more and more attractive. Moreover, with the arrival of an efficient railway network between 1850 and 1860, prairie farmers could sell their grain and livestock to distant customers without the burden of long, difficult wagon rides.
>
> There were also many innovations in farm technology during this era that made the farmer's life easier and more profitable. Two new kinds of reaping machines (developed by Hussey and McCormick, respectively) sped up the harvest and did the work of many laborers—who were always in very short supply. The harvester (which gathered grain into bundles), the self-knotting binder (which tied the bundles up), the steel plow, and other inventions all transformed prairie farming into a financially solid enterprise.

Now, on another sheet of paper, use the information in your graphic organizer to write a brief summary or a brief paraphrase of the reading. Be sure to indicate which one you are writing.

Summarizing and Paraphrasing *(continued)*

QUIZ

Complete each of the following statements, which are based on the reading about prairie farmers in the mid-nineteenth century.

1. The word *innovations* means
   (a) building new inns or hotels
   (b) newly developed things
   (c) clapping hands in an audience
   (d) producing eggs

2. The word *enterprise* in this passage means
   (a) winning a reward or prize
   (b) entering a contest
   (c) a business or project
   (d) something of great value

3. Between 1850 and 1860, farming became more profitable because
   (a) there were so many laborers to help do the farming
   (b) the Civil War kept up the demand for wheat
   (c) many farmers moved back to New York
   (d) a good railroad network was built in the Midwest

4. Eastern markets like New York probably paid high prices for Midwestern wheat because
   (a) the wheat grown in New York was not as tasty
   (b) the demand for wheat in New York was greater than the supply
   (c) Midwestern wheat was more fashionable
   (d) there were import taxes to pay

5. Improvements in farm technology in the mid-1800s meant that
   (a) planting and harvesting were done more quickly and easily
   (b) computers transformed the way the crops were grown
   (c) the farmers were soon out of jobs
   (d) most farmers went into debt buying new equipment

PART 5
Reading in Social Studies

LESSON 15
Common Features and Patterns in Social Studies Reading

Everyday Reading

What kinds of reading do you do every day? Probably more than you think. For example, when you're waiting for dinner, you might look over the newspaper headlines or TV listings. When you're shopping or banking, you probably read signs, fliers, forms, and receipts. You may read e-mail and surf the Internet. You go to school and do homework. This all requires plenty of reading.

Social Studies Reading

When you're reading for a social studies class, you are probably not reading purely for pleasure but to gather information. How much do you know about the kinds of social studies reading your teacher assigns? How can you get the most benefit out of each kind?

Social studies reading can be divided into two basic groups: **primary sources** and **secondary sources.** Primary sources include all firsthand information: eyewitness accounts of historical events, true stories (narratives) that someone tells about his or her own life, original speeches, laws, and other firsthand official documents. Secondary sources are everything else: They are other people's versions of something that has happened.

Primary Sources
- letters
- diaries
- speeches
- government proceedings
- court testimony
- oral histories
- autobiographies

Secondary Sources
- textbooks
- news reports
- magazine or journal articles
- biographies
- histories

Both broad groups are extremely important in social studies. Textbooks and other secondary sources give you the big picture about an era or a special theme in history. Diary accounts and other primary sources give you real-life details, human emotions, and unique points of view about historical events and times. For most social studies students, though, the bulk of their reading assignments are secondary sources—textbooks and other histories.

Features and Patterns To Look For

Here are some of the most common features, or special characteristics, to watch for when you read social studies assignments.

Common Features

Graphics

- maps
- charts
- graphs
- time lines
- photos
- drawings

Special Text

- bulleted/numbered lists
- boxed or shaded text
- special chapter introductions with key topics
- special chapter endings with summaries
- questions to think about
- highlighted material

Each of these features needs special attention as you read. They tell you important information that regular written text cannot convey.

Here are some of the most common patterns, or ways of organizing information, to be aware of in your social studies reading.

Common Patterns

- Chronological order
- Main idea and details
- Cause and effect
- Compare and contrast

Once you learn how to recognize and interpret these features and patterns, you can apply the best possible reading strategy to each one. This will help you master social studies material. It will also help you organize and express your thoughts better when you write. In the following lessons, we'll examine many of these common features and patterns in more detail.

LESSON 16
Maps, Photos, and Drawings

Visual Literacy

In Lesson 4, graphics were referred to as "any text elements that are not just words." Graphics are information presented in various visual forms. An old saying goes, "A picture is worth a thousand words." Graphics can be very powerful. They convey a great deal of information in an efficient manner that our eyes and brains can quickly grasp.

Literacy means the ability to read and write. It also means being able to understand what you read. In the same way, students today need to be skilled in visual literacy. This means the ability to understand and interpret visual information—to "read" graphics.

Maps

In social studies, perhaps the most important and most common graphic feature is the map. Maps show, in picture form, the relative location and size of places in the world (or in the universe). Maps can describe small areas (like the layout of rooms in a museum) or large areas (like our solar system). Most often, social studies maps show important sections of our world. They may tell us about the physical world (the geography of lands and oceans, for example) or the political world (national borders, trade routes, battles fought, and so on).

To fully understand a map, it is important to be familiar with its key elements or features.

Map Features

- compass rose—indicates direction: north, south, east, west
- legend or key—explains what different markings on the map mean
- distance indicator—shows how many miles, kilometers, and so forth, a fixed distance on the map represents
- labels—words inserted on the map to indicate special places or trails, routes, and so forth
- caption—words appearing just outside the map area that tell what the whole map is showing

Maps, Photos, and Drawings (*continued*)

Photographs

When you come to a photograph in your reading, give it your full attention. Does it show something about the subject of your reading? Does it reinforce a particular theme? Or is it just decoration? Any one of these answers could be correct, depending on the reading selection.

Also consider the photographer's bias. Just as writers have personal beliefs that can color their work, so do photographers. Photos send powerful messages, but interpret them with care.

Drawings

Drawings can take many forms, including blueprints, sketches, cartoons, and diagrams, among others. In all cases, stop and look when you see a drawing in your reading selection. Interpret it as carefully as you would a photograph. What message is the drawing meant to convey?

Application

The following reading selection includes both informational text and a map. Read the selection and study the map. Use whichever graphic organizer you wish to take notes on the passage and its graphics. Then answer the questions that follow the reading.

In the early 1800s, federal policy in the United States was to absorb, or "assimilate," Native Americans. The goal was to persuade the Indians to adopt white ways of life, and to take up farming instead of roaming the land and hunting. The Shawnee chief Tecumseh called a large group together to fight assimilation and the taking of Indian lands, but they lost the struggle at the Battle of Tippecanoe. In 1828 a new president, Andrew Jackson, decided to promote an even harsher policy: removal. His Indian Removal Act of 1830 made it legal for the United States government to move all Native Americans living on eastern lands to an "Indian Territory" west of the Mississippi River.

Some tribes resisted by going to war against the whites. The Black Hawk and Seminole Wars both took place at this time. Other tribes, like the Cherokee, tried nonviolent resistance. In the end, however, all attempts to change policy failed. The Native Americans were forced to resettle in the Indian Territory set aside for them by the federal government. These trips west (see map) were long, heartbreaking, and, in many cases, deadly for these displaced native peoples.

Adapted from *Focus on U.S. History: The Era of Expansion and Reform* by Kathy Sammis. © 1997 by J. Weston Walch, Publisher.

Maps, Photos, and Drawings (continued)

Routes taken by Native Americans affected by the Indian Removal Act of 1830

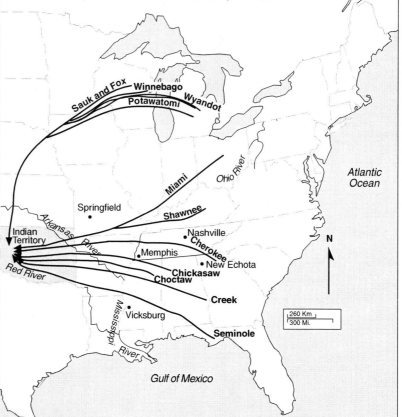

(From *Focus on U.S. History: The Era of Expansion and Reform* by Kathy Sammis, p. 100.)

1. How many Native American tribes are represented on this map? _____

2. In what state(s) does the Indian Territory appear to be? _____
   _____

3. Most of this territory lies between what two rivers? _____
   _____

4. How many states were these Native American forced to leave? _____

5. About how many miles long was the trail taken by the Miami? _____

6. About how many miles long was the trail taken by the Cherokee? _____

LESSON 17
Charts, Graphs, and Time Lines

Charts, graphs, and time lines appear often in social studies reading. What do these graphic organizers look like? What purpose does each one serve?

Charts

Charts present a group of facts about a particular topic. This information takes the form of a table or other simple diagram. A typical chart looks like this.

Paper Currency: Denomination	Front	Back
1	George Washington	"One" and U.S. Seal
2	Thomas Jefferson	Monticello*
5	Abraham Lincoln	Lincoln Memorial
10	Alexander Hamilton	U.S. Treasury
20	Andrew Jackson	White House
50	Ulysses S. Grant	U.S. Capitol
100	Benjamin Franklin	Independence Hall
500	William McKinley	"Five Hundred"
1,000	Grover Cleveland	"One Thousand"
5,000	James Madison	"Five Thousand"
10,000	Salmon P. Chase	"Ten Thousand"
50,000	Carter Glass	Spread Eagle
100,000	Woodrow Wilson	"One Hundred Thousand"

* Two-dollar bills issued beginning in 1976 have a picture of the signing of the Declaration of Independence rather than a view of Monticello on the back.

In a table chart, related facts are lined up in neat columns and rows. This visual aid helps the reader sort through the information in an orderly manner. In pie charts, different facts go into different-sized wedges of the pie. In each case, the information in a chart is sorted out visually to make more sense to the reader.

Charts, Graphs, and Time Lines *(continued)*

Graphs

Graphs are special diagrams that show changes of a variable item over time. This change is usually represented by curving lines, zigzagging lines, or bars. A typical graph looks like this.

Immigration to the United States, 1800–1866

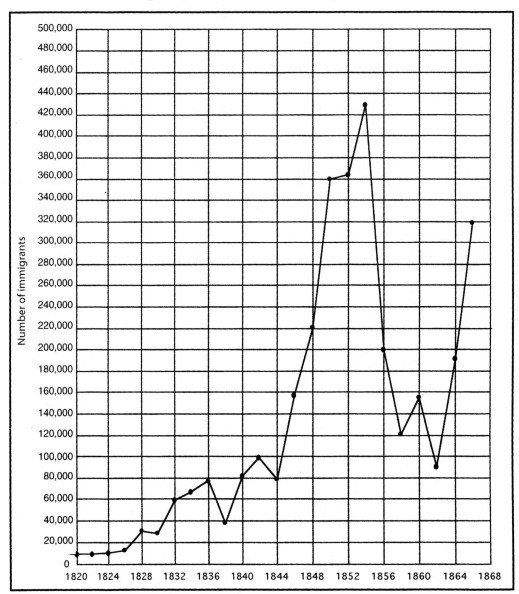

When you are reading a graph, you need to read all of the headings it contains, even if the headings are located in odd positions—like the words "Number of Immigrants" in the graph shown here. You may also need to use your index finger, a ruler, or another aid when you check the exact location of certain points on the graph line (or bar), since these points sometimes fall into "white space" on the graph (as you can see here).

Charts, Graphs, and Time Lines *(continued)*

Time Lines   The name tells it all: Time lines are graphic organizers that show time as a continuous line. Along one side of the line, important dates are noted; along the other side of the line, across from each date, a simple phrase or sentence tells what happened then. A typical time line looks like this.

Date	Events
1991	Thurgood Marshall resigned
1992	Haitian refugees returned to Haiti; Rodney King police officers tried; U.S. troops to Somalia
1993	Motor voter bill passed; World Trade Center bombing; women combat pilots approved
1994	North American Free Trade Agreement became law; U.S. troops left Somalia
1995	Million Man March; Oklahoma City bombing; U.S. planes bombed Serb positions; 20,000 U.S. troops sent to Bosnia
1996	Madeleine Albright first female Secretary of State; Welfare Reform bill
1997	
1998	President Clinton impeached by the U.S. House of Representatives
1999	U.S. returned Panama Canal to Panama; President Clinton acquitted by the U.S. Senate
2000	George W. Bush elected 43rd president of the United States
2001	Terrorists fly planes into World Trade Center and Pentagon; World Trade Center towers collapse

Time lines can be set up horizontally or vertically. The one shown here is arranged vertically; the time line runs up and down the page.

Charts, Graphs, and Time Lines *(continued)*

Application   The following reading selection includes both informational text and a graph. Read the selection and study the graph. Use whichever graphic organizer you like to record information from the reading and graphics. Then answer the questions that appear after the reading.

In the business world, manufacturers must constantly struggle between their desire to raise prices and the need to keep prices low enough to attract the largest number of buyers. When an item is priced too low, unit sales may skyrocket, yet the manufacturer makes less money. This is because the low price at which the product is selling does not fully cover the costs of manufacturing and advertising. On the other hand, when an item is priced too high, unit sales may plummet, yet the manufacturer makes a profit on the few items that are sold.

In the graph shown here, the solid line shows how the demand for widgets increases or decreases depending on the sales price. The dashed line shows how many widgets the manufacturer is willing to make as the sales price is increased or decreased. The point where the two lines cross is called the equilibrium market price—the point where supply and demand are in perfect balance.

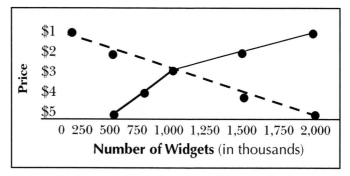

Adapted from *Understanding Our Economy* by E. Richard Churchill and Linda R. Churchill. © 1998 by J. Weston Walch, Publisher.

1. What does the dotted line on the graph show?

2. What does the solid line on the graph show?

3. The point where the two lines meet (intersect) is called what?

4. What is the ideal price for a widget, according to this graph?

5. At what point are the two lines farthest apart? Why?

LESSON 18
Chronological Order

Authors of social studies materials usually arrange their information in one of four ways. These are: (1) chronological order, (2) main idea and details, (3) cause and effect, and (4) compare and contrast. Writers will select one of these four patterns because it fits their information best and communicates their ideas most clearly.

Chronological Order

Perhaps the most straightforward of all the reading/writing patterns is chronological order. Based on two Greek words meaning "time" (*chronos*) and "speaking or reasoning" (*logikos*), chronological order lays out a series of events in the order of their occurrence. The earliest event comes first, followed by the next earliest, and so on, until the last (most recent) event is described.

Readers can learn to recognize the words and phrases that often signal chronological order. Naturally, these terms relate to time, sequence of events, or steps in a process. Here are some of the most common.

Chronological Order Words		
after	in the end	shortly thereafter
around the same time	last	simultaneously
before	later	since
during	latest	subsequently
earliest	next	succeeding (coming after)
finally	preceding (coming before)	then
first/second/third/etc.	prior to	was followed by

Application

The following selection was written to present information in chronological order. It was written by a prominent member of the community of Danvers, Massachusetts, in 1872. The writer here is giving part of the history of Danvers from his 1870s viewpoint. Read the selection, paying close attention to time and sequence words as well as dates. Then answer the questions that follow the reading.

The shoemaking industry . . . had been planted in the place [Danvers] near the beginning of the century. Before that time, shoes had been made only for home use. But new markets were opening; and the men of Danvers had the [wisdom] and energy to enter upon them. . . . The goods were mostly made of the coarser sort, for the Southern slaves. They were sent chiefly in coasting vessels [ships]; but, during the War of 1812, they were carried . . . by horse-teams fitted out from this place. . . .

In about 1835, James Goodale, Otis Mudge, and others began then to make ladies' and children's shoes of a finer grade, sending them to Boston for distribution from that point. This was done at first on a small scale; but the business has since greatly increased. In 1854 there were in the town, within its present limits, thirty-five firms engaged in this business, making annually 1,562,000 pairs, valued at $1,072,258, and giving employment to about 2,500 persons—men and women.

The use of machinery in the work has increased year by year; though the most radical changes in this respect date from about 1860. Machines are now employed at almost every step. The manual labor required has been reduced one-half. . . . Production being also carried on with greater rapidity, the workmen are usually left without employment for considerable periods in each year. [It is hoped that] this very great evil . . . will not be permanent.

From Rice, *History of the First Parish in Danvers, 1672–1872*, pp. 142–143.

1. The following events are taken from the reading above, but they are listed out of order. Number each event in its proper sequence, following the chronological order of the reading.

   (a) _____ James Goodale and Otis Mudge began to make shoes of a finer grade.

   (b) _____ Machines were being used at every step of the shoemaking process.

   (c) _____ Shoes were made for slaves in the South.

   (d) _____ Shoes were sent by horseback rather than by ship because of war.

   (e) _____ There were 35 firms involved in the shoemaking business in Danvers.

   (f) _____ Very simple shoes were made mostly to be worn in the house.

Chronological Order *(continued)*

2. Does chronological order work well in this selection? Explain your answer.

3. Why do you think chronological order is used often in informational texts?

4. In what reading/writing situations is chronological order most appropriate?

5. In what reading/writing situations is chronological order not appropriate?

6. If you had a sequence of events to describe, but you did not want to use straight chronological order in your writing, how could you order the events instead?

L ESSON 19
Main Idea and Details

Main Idea and Details

Many social studies readings are not based on a particular sequence of events (as in chronological order). Instead, the focus may be on a special theme or subject—like America's reasons for entering World War II, social life in a frontier town, or Native American hunting techniques. In these cases, authors often choose to present their information using main idea and details.

How do you know when your reading is organized according to main idea and details? You can probably figure this out by reading the first paragraph or two and looking for a **topic sentence.** This is the sentence that spells out the topic or idea that the writer is focusing on—the main idea. Many of the surrounding sentences support this main topic or idea; they give further information about it. These are the sentences providing the details.

Topic sentence = Main idea

Supporting sentences = Details

It is important to remember that the main idea does not always come first. Often, of course, the topic sentence will appear at the very beginning of a paragraph. At other times, however, the topic sentence may be sandwiched into the middle of a paragraph, or it may appear at the end of the paragraph.

Remember, too, that there may be more than one main idea, especially if the reading passage contains more than one or two paragraphs. Generally speaking, each new paragraph introduces a new thought. Therefore, readers need to examine each paragraph to see whether it contains a brand-new topic sentence, or whether it is continuing to support the topic sentence in the preceding paragraph.

Application

The following selection presents information according to a main-idea-and-details pattern. Read the selection, looking closely for topic sentences and supporting sentences. Then answer the questions that appear after the reading.

Main Idea and Details *(continued)*

Most of the ancient Greeks worshipped the same gods (or deities). These were the gods of Mount Olympus. Yet, from town to town, there was a wide variety in the form this worship took. The Greeks had no official religious documents or books (like the Bible or the Koran). Therefore, they simply followed the religious customs of their local communities. They visited their temples as individuals, making special offerings or prayers as needed. They also celebrated together at religious festivals, which were often rather rowdy social events. In short, the Greeks had no central religious authority and no formal creed, or set of beliefs.

The ancient Greek gods were closely tied to nature and daily family life. Zeus, the king of the gods, was often considered a father figure. Poseidon ruled the oceans, making calm seas or ferocious storms for the Greek sailors to navigate. Aphrodite, goddess of love and beauty, helped—or inter-fered—in the romantic lives of young men and women. The wild god Pan protected the flocks of sheep and goats that many Greek families depended on for survival.

1. The following sentences can be found in the reading above. For each sentence, indicate whether it represents a main idea or a detail. Write **MI** for main idea and **D** for detail.

   (a) Yet, from town to town, there was a wide variety in the form this worship took. _____

   (b) The Greeks had no official religious documents or books (like the Bible or the Koran). _____

   (c) In short, the Greeks had no central religious authority and no formal creed, or set of beliefs. _____

   (d) Zeus, the king of the gods, was often considered a father figure. _____

   (e) Most of the ancient Greeks worshipped the same gods (or deities). _____

   (f) The wild god Pan protected the flocks of sheep and goats that many Greek families depended on for survival. _____

   (g) The ancient Greek gods were closely tied to nature and daily family life. _____

   (h) They visited their temples as individuals, making special offerings or prayers as needed. _____

2. How many topic sentences did you find in this passage?

3. For each topic sentence that you identified, describe its location.

4. Which location do you prefer for a topic sentence? Why?

LESSON 20
Cause and Effect

Cause and Effect

When authors want to tell how one event in history triggered other events, or how the climate of a particular country affects its agriculture, or how high demand for a new product can create shortages and higher prices, for example, they organize their information to show cause and effect. Cause and effect shows how one condition or event results in another.

Think of a set of dominoes, standing on their ends and arranged neatly in a row. Your finger— or a gust of wind, or the wagging tail of a dog—hits the first domino in the row. It begins to fall. This is cause and effect. Then, the first domino hits the second one as it falls; the second domino falls, too—and then the third, the fourth, and so on down the row. This type of chain reaction—a whole series of events rather than just one—can also be shown using the cause-and-effect pattern.

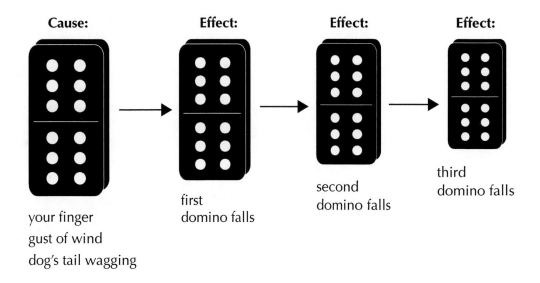

Cause:

your finger
gust of wind
dog's tail wagging

Effect:

first
domino falls

Effect:

second
domino falls

Effect:

third
domino falls

Order

It is important to keep in mind that the cause does not always come first in the reading. The cause may appear in the middle or at the end of a paragraph, too. When this happens, the effects come first in the reading. You need to read through the effects to arrive at their cause.

© 2002 J. Weston Walch, Publisher

Content-Area Reading Strategies: Social Studies

Cause and Effect (continued)

Here are some common words and phrases to look for in a passage containing cause and effect.

Cause and Effect Words		
affect	effect	lead to
bring about	impact	result
cause	influence	trigger

Remember, there may be more than one effect for each cause. Think of the dominoes and the chain reaction. Also, there may be more than one cause. Think, for example, of World War II and the various factors that caused the United States to join that conflict.

Application The following selection presents information according to the cause-and-effect pattern. Read the selection carefully. Then answer the questions that follow the reading.

> In 1874 came a giant calamity in the form of a raid of grasshoppers which ate up every bit of green vegetation from the Rocky Mountains to and beyond the Missouri River. I recall that when coming home late one afternoon for supper I stepped back surprised to see what became known as Rocky Mountain locusts covering the side of the house. Already inside, they feasted on the curtains. Clouds of them promptly settled down on the whole country—everywhere, unavoidable. People set about killing them to save gardens, but this soon proved ridiculous. . . . Vast hordes, myriads. In a week grain fields, gardens, shrubs, vines, had been eaten down to the ground or to the bark. Nothing could be done. You sat by and saw everything go.
>
> When autumn came with the country devastated, the population despaired again when seeing the insects remaining for the winter with the apparent plan of being on hand for the next season. . . .
>
> From Stuart Henry, *Conquering Our Great American Plains*. New York: E.P. Dutton & Co., Inc. 1930. As found in Commager and Nevins, eds., *The Heritage of America*, p. 861.

1. The passage above describes the great grasshopper plague of 1874. The author has described some of the immediate effects of the grasshopper infestation. There are other effects, however, that you can probably infer (reason out) from the reading. For example, what happens when a whole year's crop is wiped out? How does that affect both the growers of the crop and the people who are expecting to buy it?

Cause and Effect *(continued)*

Finish the cause-and-effect chart below, adding as many effects from the reading and from your inferences as possible.

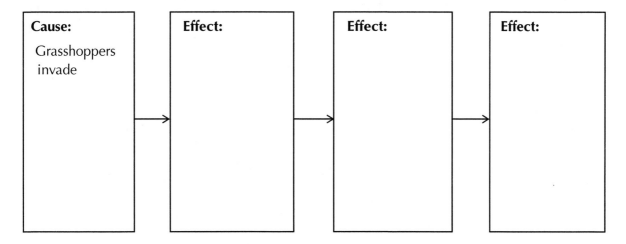

Cause:		Effect:		Effect:		Effect:
Grasshoppers invade	→		→		→	

2. Does organizing information by showing cause and effect help you remember what you read? Why or why not?

3. Think of your social studies themes and topics at school this year. In which cases do you think arranging the material to show cause and effect would be most useful?

LESSON 21
Compare and Contrast

Comparing and Contrasting

When we compare one person or thing with another, we are looking for ways in which they are similar. When we contrast someone or something with another, we are looking for ways in which they are different. By identifying both the similarities and the differences, we are seeing both sides of a subject, with the goal of understanding it better.

In the world of social studies, authors use comparing and contrasting as a way to organize information for many reasons, including

- to show differing beliefs or actions between key people in history
- to describe the conflicting viewpoints of two or more political groups, countries, and so on
- to relate one civilization or culture to another
- to show how something has changed over time (before/after)

Here are some common words used to compare and contrast.

Compare Words	Contrast Words
equal	contrary
identical	different/differing
in comparison	in contrast
like	on the other hand
resemble	opposite/opposing
same	unlike
similar/similarly	

Application

The following selection was written to compare and contrast information. Read the selection carefully, using a graphic organizer. Then answer the questions that follow the reading.

Compare and Contrast *(continued)*

The Anasazi culture first took root sometime around the beginning of the Common Era. These Pueblo Indian peoples inhabited what is now New Mexico and Arizona. In the one thousand years between the first and third phases of their culture, several significant developments occurred.

In their first stage of civilization, the Anasazi lived in caves or in small, round adobe huts. They hunted with flint-headed spears and grew a species of small corn for food. They wove simple baskets for containers and smoked tobacco. Other than in winter, when they wore furs, they were naked except for sandals on their feet.

By the time of their third phase of civilization, the Anasazi lived in networks of cliff dwellings that were difficult for enemies to attack. Their buildings were terraced—much like some modern skyscrapers—and their basket weaving, now in black-on-white designs, had reached a new level of sophistication. They wove fabrics for clothing and wore jewelry made of shells, seeds, and turquoise. For weapons they now used bows and arrows.

1. Complete the graphic organizer below, using information from the reading about the Anasazi. Compare and contrast features of the first and third stages of their civilization. Two categories have been included. Add the other appropriate categories yourself.

Category	First Stage (around 1 c.e.)	Third Stage (around 1000 c.e.)
Housing		
Weapons		

2. Does organizing information in the compare-and-contrast pattern help you remember what you read?

3. Think of your social studies themes and topics at school this year. In which cases do you think comparing and contrasting would be most useful?

4. Are there other organizational patterns you might use to arrange the material in this reading about the Anasazi?

LESSON 22
Review

In the previous lessons, you have studied—and applied—some powerful new strategies to use in your social studies reading. Now, you will have the opportunity to practice these new reading strategies with some longer reading selections. First, let's review what you've learned.

The Reading Process

There are three stages in effective reading: (1) prereading, (2) reading, (3) postreading. Each of these stages involves specific steps. If you follow these steps when you read, you learn and remember much more.

Prereading (before reading) 4 Ps	Reading	Postreading (after reading)
Preview Predict Prior knowledge Purpose	**Using graphic organizers:** **KWL** (what I **K**now; what I **W**ant to know; what I have **L**earned) **SQ3R** (Survey, Question, Read, Recall, Reflect) **Semantic web** **Outline** **Structured notes**	**ALWAYS either:** **Summarize** (using words from text) OR **Paraphrase** (using your own words)

Common Reading/ Writing Patterns in Social Studies

Learn to recognize these patterns and you'll become a stronger, more independent reader.

Chronological Order	Main Idea/ Details	Cause and Effect	Compare/ Contrast
Time—events laid out in sequence, in order as they happened	**Main idea** = topic sentence **Details** = sentences that support main idea Main idea doesn't always come first in reading!	**Cause** triggers other events (**Effects**). Cause doesn't always come first in reading!	**Compare** = what's *similar* **Contrast** = what's *different* 2 or more things/ people examined

PART 6
Practice Readings

READING A

Use a graphic organizer to record important information in the selection below. Read the selection carefully, making notes as you read. When you have finished, be sure to write a brief summary or paraphrase of the material. Then check your understanding by taking the quiz that follows the reading.

Dynastic Rule in Egypt

At about the same time that Mesopotamia was being settled by the Sumerians, ancient Egypt was being united under one ruler. King Menes, one of a group of powerful chieftains from the south, unified Upper and Lower Egypt in about 3100 B.C.E. He built his capital at Memphis (near present-day Cairo) and began the dynasty system—royal rulers who descended within families. In all, during the millennia between 3100 and 343 B.C.E., thirty dynasties—roughly corresponding to thirty royal family groups—ruled Egypt.

The history of the dynastic period is traditionally divided into three major eras, or kingdoms: the Old Kingdom, from 2686 to 2181 B.C.E. (first through third dynasties); the Middle Kingdom, from 1991 to 1786 B.C.E. (eleventh through thirteenth dynasties); and the New Kingdom, from 1570 to 1070 B.C.E. (eighteenth through twentieth dynasties). Between the end of the Old Kingdom and the beginning of the Middle, the First Intermediate Period occurred. This period was marked by weak kings, chronic unrest, and divided rule within the kingdom. Likewise, between the end of the Middle Kingdom and the beginning of the New, the Second Intermediate Period took place—again marked by divided rule and ineffective leadership. A final period (the twenty-first through thirtieth dynasties) following the New Kingdom was marked by foreign invasions, fragmentation, and ultimately conquest by Alexander the Great in 334 B.C.E.

The Old Kingdom marked a period of general prosperity, artistic accomplishment, and the development of formal religion. It was during this period that the Egyptians began building pyramids out of native limestone and granite. The first of these was erected during the third dynasty in the reign of Zoser. Perhaps the oldest monument remaining on Earth today, this stepped pyramid is located near Memphis (the capital of the Old Kingdom), flanked by shrines and other related buildings. However, the most famous pyramid from this era is the Great Pyramid of Khufu at Giza. Built in about 2600 B.C.E. , this architectural marvel was made from approximately 2.3 million stone blocks, all meticulously put in place without cranes, pulleys, or other lifting equipment considered a necessity today.

(continued)

Dynastic Rule in Egypt (continued)

The first king of the Middle Kingdom was Mentuhotep II of the eleventh dynasty. Following the troubled First Intermediate Period, Mentuhotep was one of a line of strong rulers from Thebes who once again united the kingdom. During the Middle Kingdom, Egyptian territory expanded. The arts also thrived once more. Sculpture of this era shows greater efforts at realism, and jewelry making reached new heights of sophistication. Artisans used precious metals and colored stones to fashion both personal adornments and figurines. The best known of these may be the small blue-glazed hippopotamus often replicated today for sale in museum stores.

After the Second Intermediate Period, which saw the invasion of Hyksos from western Asia, the New Kingdom began with the return of strong rulers from Thebes. During this era, the empire again expanded—primarily through foreign conquests—and the kingdom was known for its power and wealth. Ancient Egyptian civilization reached its pinnacle in the New Kingdom, particularly during the reign of Thutmose III. Its territory stretched throughout the Middle East, from Ethiopia to Syria. The temple complex at Al Karnak, one of the most imposing religious structures in history, was built during the New Kingdom period. Also erected around this time was the temple at Abu Simbel in Nubia, built for Ramses II of the nineteenth dynasty. This temple, placed in the Valley of the Kings burial site, is cut into the rock and carved with colossal figures. Sculpture of the New Kingdom shows more delicacy and detail, and tomb paintings are extremely vivid and revealing, showing many important aspects of daily life in ancient Egypt.

QUIZ: Dynastic Rule in Egypt

Circle the letter of the answer that best completes each sentence.

1. The Egyptian dynasty system is based on
   (a) the descendants of King Menes
   (b) rule by royal families
   (c) descendants of Alexander the Great
   (d) residents of the Old Kingdom

2. The dynastic period consisted of
   (a) three major dynasties
   (b) twenty dynasties
   (c) thirty dynasties
   (d) over a hundred dynasties

3. The Old Kingdom was noted for
   (a) the first pyramids
   (b) fine jewelry making
   (c) weak kings and divided rule
   (d) foreign invasion

4. The word *chronic* means
   (a) telling time
   (b) constant, continuing
   (c) a written story
   (d) extremely painful

5. In this reading, times of weak rule are linked with
   (a) a divided empire
   (b) improved sculpture and other arts
   (c) expansion of territory
   (d) higher taxes

READING B

Use a graphic organizer to record important information in the selection below. Read the selection carefully, making notes as you read. When you have finished, be sure to write a brief summary or paraphrase of the material. Then check your understanding by taking the quiz that follows the reading.

The Effect of Environment on Mesopotamian Culture

The term *Mesopotamia* is derived from two ancient Greek words: *mesos* (middle) and *potamus* (river). Certainly, the name is an appropriate one, since Mesopotamia was the area of land sandwiched in between two major rivers of the Near East: the Tigris and the Euphrates. Both rivers have their headwaters in the Armenian mountains (now part of Turkey), and both—along with the climate and terrain that characterize this region of the world—have heavily influenced the history and culture of the ancient peoples living near their banks.

Mesopotamia was first settled by the Sumerians, who began farming the flat lands in the south sometime before 3000 B.C.E. Their agricultural efforts were successful mainly because the Sumerians were able to establish irrigation and drainage systems that linked their fields to the rivers. In addition to the abundant crops this fertile soil produced, the rivers were filled with fish—a staple in the Mesopotamian diet—and the marshlands beyond the riverbanks offered plenty of wildfowl.

The Sumerians also established the first cities in this area. Recognizing the importance of the rivers for their survival, they selected sites for the major settlements of Ur and Uruk on tributaries of the Euphrates; for the city of Lagash they chose a site on one of the branches of the Tigris. From these centers, the Sumerians used the rivers for travel, trade, and communication, as well as for lines of defense when under attack. Again, the rivers provided the necessities of life, including the all-important mud and reeds for their building materials, since there is little stone in the region.

The rivers could also be obstacles, however. For example, the complex of waterways formed by the Tigris and Euphrates, their tributaries, and the many irrigation canals built along their banks, broke Mesopotamia up into numerous fragments. Cities therefore tended to be isolated. Rather than uniting the entire region under one government and forming a common defense, they instead became individual city-states. This made each one more vulnerable to invasion from both

(continued)

The Effect of Environment on Mesopotamian Culture (continued)

the nomadic tribes wandering the deserts and swamps between the settlements and from other city-states. There was a nearly constant state of warfare among the Sumerian cities for centuries.

Flooding was also a recurring problem. When the rivers overflowed their banks, they were capable of destroying entire settlements. In fact, one ancient Sumerian myth concerns a catastrophic flood that may have had a basis in reality. This myth most likely was the source of the biblical story of Noah, the ark, and the great flood.

QUIZ: The Effect of Environment on Mesopotamian Culture

Circle the letter of the answer that best completes each sentence.

1. Mesopotamia is the region located
   (a) in the Armenian mountains (now Turkey)
   (b) near the ancient Greek settlement of Euphrates
   (c) between tributaries of the Tigris River
   (d) between the Tigris and Euphrates rivers

2. The Sumerians became successful farmers largely because
   (a) they used the rivers for irrigation
   (b) they had learned so much from the Greeks
   (c) nomadic tribes in the area provided inexpensive labor
   (d) the federal government gave them financial help

3. Common foods in the Sumerian diet included
   (a) fish and wild birds
   (b) wild boar and birds
   (c) fish and maize
   (d) vegetables and wild birds

4. The word *recurring* means
   (a) running backwards; reversing direction
   (b) happening again and again
   (c) retreating or withdrawing
   (d) needing a great deal of courage

5. Based on this reading, you might assume that unifying Mesopotamia
   (a) was a top priority for the Sumerians
   (b) was made easier by the Tigris and Euphrates rivers
   (c) took a relatively short time
   (d) took a relatively long time

READING C

Use a graphic organizer to record important information in the selection below. Read the selection carefully, making notes as you read. When you have finished, be sure to write a brief summary or paraphrase of the material. Then check your understanding by taking the quiz that follows the reading.

The Growth of Towns in the Middle Ages

There is probably no one explanation for the evolution of medieval towns, although most scholars believe that a common need for defense played an important role in the process. No matter what the reasons for their origins, however, all towns of the early Middle Ages (twelfth and thirteenth centuries) shared several key characteristics. For example, all early towns were enclosed by walls to prevent, or at least discourage, invasion. As a town grew, new walls were simply put up to accommodate the larger area. In addition, all medieval towns had a marketplace, a vital center of communication and trade, usually located in the heart of the community. They also had a court, where disputes were settled, and a mint, where money was coined.

As well as sharing these physical and institutional features, early medieval towns also shared a human feature: a new class of tradespeople. These merchants and artisans, originally of peasant stock, were responsible for creating what later became known as the middle class. Unlike both the nobility and the peasants, they were not tied to the land. Nor, in general, were they as concerned about church matters; they were becoming more interested in worldly things. In fact, many townspeople were viewed by those who remained in the country as living more luxurious lives. Although most residents of medieval towns were actually far from wealthy, there certainly was an increasing belief in business for its own sake. In other words, rather than simply bartering to exchange necessary goods, people began to believe that making a profit could be a desirable goal.

The earliest medieval towns were usually located on land that was owned by a lord, who required payment for the use of his property. As a result, a tax system developed at the town gates, so that anyone entering town to buy or sell goods paid a fee before entering. Much of this money went directly to the lord, but some of the remaining funds went to the town council. Citizens of the town were exempt from this tax, as were runaway serfs who could manage to live in town for a year and a day without getting caught. Such individuals then became citizens, too, who could buy and sell goods without paying

(continued)

The Growth of Towns in the Middle Ages **(continued)**

tolls and taxes like the "foreigners." In this way, people from the country were encouraged to leave their lives of drudgery and join the growing populations in the towns.

One of the most significant developments in the history of towns in the early Middle Ages was the development of the guild system. The first guilds arose out of a need for merchants who engaged in foreign trade to band together and protect themselves against bad investments or dishonest traders. These were known as the merchant guilds. At about the same time, the artisans and craftsmen of particular trades also began coming together to form their own power blocks; these were known as craft guilds. Guilds decided on the quantity, quality, and prices of the goods they created. They also decided on the number of apprentices and journeymen who could belong to their organizations. Eventually, the merchant guilds became very powerful. Their political and financial clout gradually eroded that of the lords, so that towns became more independent and more influential.

QUIZ: The Growth of Towns in the Middle Ages

Circle the letter of the answer that best completes each sentence.

1. Early medieval towns had all of the following except
   (a) a university
   (b) a mint
   (c) a surrounding wall
   (d) a court

2. Towns in the early Middle Ages had a new class of people who were
   (a) clerics (religious officials)
   (b) peasants
   (c) tradespeople
   (d) tax collectors

3. The lord in the area near the town usually
   (a) sent his peasants to the town to become citizens
   (b) tried to get the merchants in town to become farmers
   (c) invited the merchants to the castle to trade goods
   (d) wanted payment for use of the land the town was on

4. Medieval towns decreased the power of the lords; this was probably because
   (a) the lords charged higher prices for the same goods
   (b) town residents took over the lords' castles
   (c) the lords left their estates in order to live and trade in town
   (d) town residents no longer needed the lords' protection to survive

5. The word *drudgery* means
   (a) being resentful or angry at someone else
   (b) hard, tiresome work
   (c) digging up earth that lies under a body of water
   (d) being very religious

 Content-Area Reading Strategies: Social Studies

READING D

Use a graphic organizer to record important information in the selection below. Read the selection carefully, making notes as you read. When you have finished, be sure to write a brief summary or paraphrase of the material. Then check your understanding by taking the quiz that follows.

Conflicting Views of Slavery

In 1835, a young man from Maine named Joseph Holt Ingraham went south to teach at Jefferson College in Mississippi. He remained in the South for the rest of his life, dying just before the Civil War erupted. An Episcopal minister and prolific romance writer, Ingraham also authored a two-volume work on Mississippi and the neighboring area. He portrayed an idealized South in which master and slave lived in harmony, with the slave owner showing a gallant, fatherly interest in his African-American charges.

Passage A

Planters, particularly native planters [those born in the South], have a kind of affection for their Negroes, incredible to those who have not observed its effects. If rebellious they punish them—if well behaved, they not infrequently reward them. In health they treat them with uniform kindness, in sickness with attention and sympathy. . . . They are well fed and warmly clothed in the winter, in warm jackets and trousers, and blanket coats enveloping the whole person, with hats or woolen caps and brogans [heavy work shoes]. In summer they have clothing suitable to the season, and a ragged Negro is less frequently to be met with than in Northern cities.

. . . On those plantations which have no chapel and no regular worship on the Sabbath, Negroes are permitted to go to the nearest town to church, a privilege they seldom know how to appreciate, and prefer converting their liberty into an opportunity for marketing or visiting. Experience, however, has convinced planters that no indulgence to their slaves is so detrimental as this, both to the moral condition of the slave and the good order of the plantation, for there is no vice in which many of them will not become adepts, if allowed a temporary freedom from restraint one day in seven. Hence, this liberty, except in particular instances, is denied them on some estates, to which they are confined under easy discipline during the day, passing the time in strolling through the woods, sleeping, eating, and idling about the quarters. The evenings of the Sabbath are passed in little gossiping circles in some of the cabins, or beneath the shade of some tree in front of their dwellings, or at weddings. . . .

From Joseph Holt Ingraham, *The South-West by a Yankee*. New York: Harper & Brothers, 1835. As appears in Commager and Nevins, eds. *The Heritage of America*, pp. 462–464.

(continued)

Conflicting Views of Slavery (continued)

Ingraham's descriptions present a dramatically different version of life on Southern plantations from the picture painted by Fanny (Frances) Kemble at about the same time. Kemble was an English actress who married a southern planter from Georgia. Although her husband's plantation had an excellent reputation and was believed to be very well managed, Kemble was horrified by the condition of the slaves.

Passage B

In the afternoon I made my first visit to the hospital of the estate, and found it, as indeed I find everything else here, in a far worse state even than [the worse institution] . . .; so miserable a place for the purpose to which it was dedicated I could not have imagined on a property belonging to Christian owners. The floor (which was not boarded, but merely the damp hard earth itself) was strewn with wretched women, who, but for their moans of pain and uneasy restless motions, might very well have each been taken for a mere heap of filthy rags. . . . My eyes, unaccustomed to the turbid [cloudy] atmosphere, smarted and watered and refused to distinguish [see] at first the different dismal forms from which cries and wails assailed me in every corner of the place. By degrees I was able to endure for a few minutes what they were condemned to live their hours and days of suffering and sickness through; and . . . I went on to what seemed a yet more wretched abode [house] of wretchedness. There was a room where there was no fire because there was no chimney and where the holes made for windows had no panes or glasses in them. The shutters being closed, the place was so dark that, on first entering it, I was afraid to stir lest I should fall over some of the deplorable creatures extended upon the floor. As soon as they perceived [saw] me, one cry of "Oh, missis!" rang through the darkness, and it really seemed to me as if I was never to exhaust the pity and amazement and disgust which this receptacle of suffering humanity was to excite in me. . . .

I promised them help and comfort, beds and blankets, and light and fire— that is, I promised to ask Mr. ——— for all this for them; and in the very act of doing so I remembered with a sudden pang of anguish that I was to urge no more petitions for his slaves to their master. I groped my way out, and emerging on the piazza [porch], all the choking tears and sobs I had controlled burst forth. . .

From Frances Anne Kemble, *Journal of a Residence on a Georgian Plantation in 1838–1839*. New York: Harper & Brothers, 1863. As found in Commager and Nevins, eds., *The Heritage of America*, pp. 465–466.

QUIZ: Conflicting Views of Slavery

Circle the letter of the answer that best completes each sentence.

1. In Ingraham's account of plantation life, all of the following are true except
   (a) slaves were treated kindly and fairly by their masters
   (b) slaves who were ill received care and attention
   (c) on Sundays, all slaves were allowed to go wherever they liked
   (d) Sunday evenings were spent chatting, strolling, and relaxing

2. In Kemble's description of plantation life,
   (a) most slaves led very happy lives
   (b) slaves who were ill received no decent medical care
   (c) slaves who were very ill were sent to good local hospitals
   (d) the hospital room was shabby and dark but well ventilated (aired)

3. The word *deplorable* means
   (a) carefully arranged
   (b) used up
   (c) very bad, highly regrettable
   (d) lying on the floor

4. These two accounts differ greatly, probably because
   (a) Kemble and Ingraham had different political and social ideas
   (b) they were written at very different times in history
   (c) Kemble was from the North (the Union) and disliked the South
   (d) Ingraham ran a cotton plantation and supported slavery

5. From this reading, we can assume that Kemble is not allowed to ask her husband for any more favors for the slaves because
   (a) she has already done so many times, and he has lost patience
   (b) he has already spent too much money improving their health care
   (c) she knows that he will be freeing them soon anyway
   (d) she is exaggerating their poor condition

Blank
Graphic
Organizers

4-P Chart

1. Preview	2. Predict	3. Prior Knowledge	4. Purpose

KWL Chart

K What I KNOW	W What I WANT to Know	L What I LEARNED

SQ3R Chart

S Survey	Q Question	R Read	R Recall	R Reflect

Content-Area Reading Strategies: Social Studies

Semantic Web

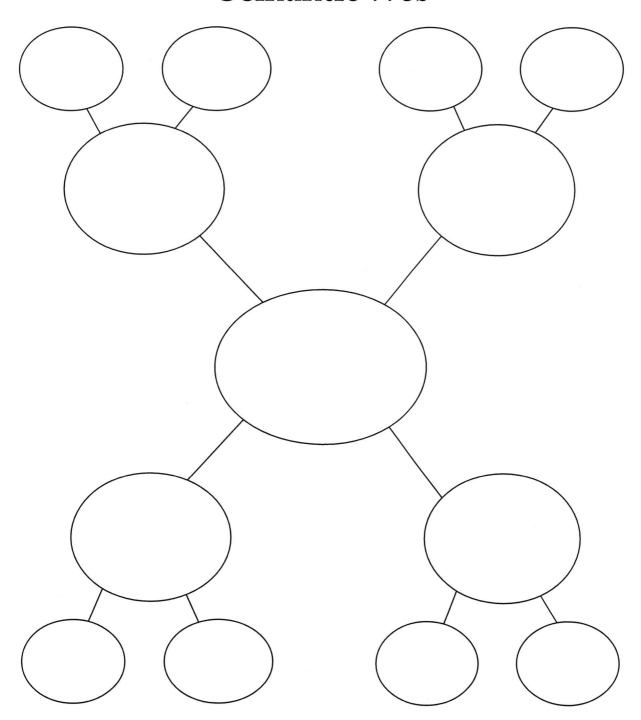

Outline

I. _____

    A. _____

        1. _____

        2. _____

        3. _____

    B. _____

        1. _____

        2. _____

        3. _____

II. _____

    A. _____

    B. _____

    C. _____

Structured Notes (some options)

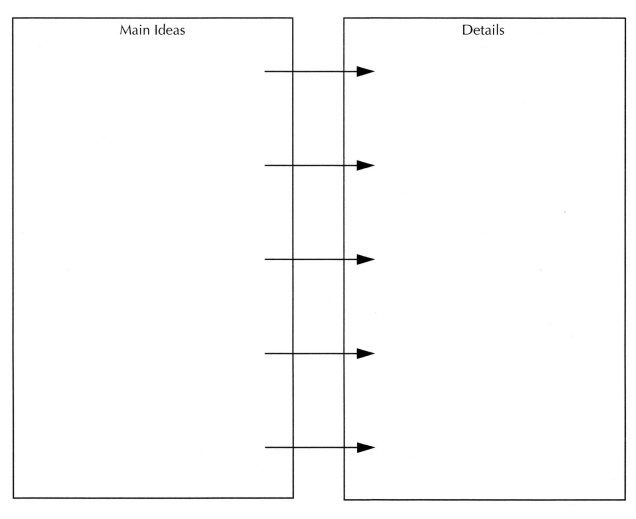

Main Ideas	Details

Events:

Dates:

Teacher's Guide
and
Answer Key

Part 1: Building Vocabulary

Lesson 1: Using Context Clues

To introduce this publication and this lesson, begin a classroom discussion about individual students' reading attitudes. What do they like about reading? What kinds of reading do they like best, and why? In many cases, students will reveal that they prefer reading for pleasure, since there is less pressure involved than when they are reading for instructional purposes. A number of students may say that they dislike encountering unfamiliar words when they read, since it slows down reading, inhibits information flow, and often entails looking the terms up in a dictionary—a generally tedious process. Explain to the class that this lesson will help them get more out of every kind of reading they do, and that it will also help them master unfamiliar words in a less disruptive manner, with less time spent for dictionary "pit stops."

To extend the lesson, have students bring to class examples of reading material they find challenging. As a group, tackle one or two unfamiliar vocabulary words using the context clue strategies they have learned in Lesson 1, and any other strategies you may wish to introduce.

Application

Answers will vary, but should include the following information:

1. *dignitary:* someone of importance and high position. Examples in the text include "wealthy businessman," "important figure," and "referred to as Deacon."
2. *treatise:* a methodical written discussion or argument. Context clue is a definition found in the text: "powerful written argument."
3. *doctrine:* clearly stated principle or position in a belief system (or government policy). Context clue is a synonym: "position."
4. *Caucus:* a meeting of like-minded individuals who select political candidates and establish policy. Context clue is a restatement: "This was a secret organization that met in advance of all town meetings to decide upon the slate of candidates for office and what the stands would be on various issues."

Lesson 2: Prefixes and Suffixes

You can extend this lesson by having students find examples of words containing prefixes and suffixes in their own reading—for example, in their social studies texts. Student volunteers can write their selected words on the board, highlighting the prefixes/suffixes and explaining how they arrived at the appropriate word meanings.

Application

Answers to the second part of each question will vary. Some possible answers are given here. 1. (a); prefix *un-* ("not") 2. (c); suffixes *-ish* ("having the characteristics of") and *-ly* ("in such a manner") 3. (b); prefix *sub-* ("below") 4. (d); prefix *ex-* ("out from") 5. (b); prefix *in-* ("not") and suffix *-ible* ("able to be")

Lesson 3: Word Forms

You can extend this lesson by dividing students into teams, then writing a "core" word or a root word on the board. Teams can compete to see how many different forms of the word they can come up with. If teams are having a difficult time with this concept, you can take away the competitive aspect of the activity and simply work together using dictionaries to come up with their answers.

Application

1. (a) ; core word: tend
2. (d); core word: territory
3. (a); core word: necessary
4. (b); core word: ally (a noun)
5. (b); core word: diminish

Encourage students who need help with the definitions to use the dictionary or to work in pairs to work these meanings out.

Part 2: Prereading

Lesson 4: Previewing

You may reinforce students' prereading skills by having them use their actual social studies texts. They can apply these strategies either to the chapter they are now working with or to an upcoming chapter.

Application

Answers will vary, but should include the following information:

1. The title tells us that the main topic pertains to growth of a new nation. It also tells us what time period is being covered (nineteenth century), but does not give the country's name.
2. The two subheadings reveal the two main themes: physical expansion and technological improvements (pertaining to both transportation and communication).
3. Boldfaced words are roads, canals, steamship, National Road, Erie Canal, *Clermont* (again, all pertaining to transportation and communication).
4. The first paragraph describes the doubling of U.S. territory by the early nineteenth century. The middle paragraphs describe transportation and communication issues resulting from such an immense expansion of territory and the solutions that were arrived at to address those issues. The final paragraph focuses on the dawn of steam transportation.
5. Graphic elements are the time line and the steamship drawing. The time line contains many references to inventions and technological developments. The drawing highlights one of the major new developments in transportation of that era.

Lesson 5: Predicting

Again, have students use their actual social studies texts or other current classroom materials to practice their prereading strategies in everyday context.

Application

Answers will vary, but should include the following information:

1. Readers should be able to predict that this passage is about the transportation and the communication issues facing early nineteenth-century America and what

improvements and innovations resolved them.

2. This passage focuses primarily on territorial expansion (first paragraph), the need for better transportation and communication (all paragraphs), the National Road (third paragraph), canals (fourth paragraph), and steamships (last paragraph).
3. Answers will vary.
4. The main idea might be that American innovation and new technology successfully met the transportation and communication challenges of an expanding nation.

Lesson 6: Prior Knowledge

Students—especially those who lack confidence—tend to underestimate the amount of prior knowledge they really have. Encourage them to think about their own personal experiences and previous reading about a given topic as you introduce it in class. They will eventually become more confident as they realize how much they really know.

Application

All answers will vary.

Lesson 7: Purpose

Author purpose and author bias are extremely important concepts for students to understand, since many readers assume that whatever they see on a printed page or on a computer screen is inherently "true." Use a newspaper to explain the difference between an opinion piece (like an editorial), which reveals bias, and a straight news story, which is generally more balanced and objective. You and your students can find many more examples showing different kinds of author bias both in print and on the Web.

Application

1. Answers will vary.
2. Answers will vary, but should include the following: The author's purpose was most likely to teach. (NOTE: You might choose to address author bias here. The author of this passage is clearly disposed to think highly of both American territorial expansion and its innovative spirit; the tone is very upbeat.)

Part 3: Reading Strategies

Lesson 8: Introduction to Reading Strategies

To reinforce each of these reading strategies and to familiarize students with the use of graphic organizers, try applying each strategy to a chapter in your social studies text. You may choose to do this together as a whole-class activity, or you may want to assign it as homework or as a small-group project.

Lesson 9: KWL

Application

All answers will vary.

Quiz

1. (d) 2. (b) 3. (d) 4. (c) 5. (a)

Lesson 10: SQ3R

Application

All answers will vary.

Quiz

1. (c) 2. (a) 3. (d) 4. (c) 5. (a)

Lesson 11: Semantic Web

Application

All answers will vary, but semantic webs created by students should include at least some of the following:

Main idea: African Americans helped the Union win the Civil War.

Details: About 200,000 escaped slaves were paid laborers for Union during war.

Many black regiments fought heroically—like 54th Massachusetts Regiment's attack on Fort Wagner.

186,000 African-American soldiers in Union army; 29,000 in navy; 38,000 died.

Fought in at least 39 major battles and 400 smaller fights.

Other African Americans helped as spies, scouts, nurses, teachers.

Quiz

1. (b) 2. (a) 3. (b) 4. (d) 5. (d)

Lesson 12: Outline

Application

Answers will vary, but a completed outline might look like this:

Hawaiian Islands

I. Geography
    A. Created well over 1000 yrs ago
    B. Volcanic islands
        1. lava from volcanoes under ocean floor
        2. stretch over hundreds of miles
        3. No near neighbors
            (a) Aleutian Islands 2000 miles north
            (b) Marquesas Islands 2000 miles south

II. Settlement/Culture
    A. Founded by Polynesians from other South Pacific islands
        1. arrived over 1000 years ago
    B. Unique Hawaiian culture developed
        1. no foreigners until Capt. Cook, 1778

Quiz

1. (b) 2. (c) 3. (d) 4. (d) 5. (a)

Lesson 13: Structured Notes

Application

Answers will vary.

Quiz

1. (a) 2. (a) 3. (d) 4. (c) 5. (d)

Part 4: Postreading

Lesson 14: Summarizing and Paraphrasing

Have students practice summarizing versus paraphrasing as they use their actual social studies texts. You might also select some well-known primary source documents (like the Preamble to the Constitution or the Gettysburg Address) and have students summarize and/or paraphrase them. If this is proving difficult for some learners, you can assign the activity as group work.

Application

All answers will vary.

Quiz

1. (b) 2. (c) 3. (d) 4. (b) 5. (a)

Part 5: Reading in Social Studies

Lesson 15: Common Features and Patterns in Social Studies Reading

This lesson introduces features and patterns that distinguish social studies texts from other texts. This is a good time to discuss primary versus secondary sources.

Lesson 16: Maps, Photos, and Drawings

As you introduce this lesson, be sure to point out common map features using examples from your classroom and from students' social studies texts. You can also bring in newspapers and news-magazines so that students can study the photos that have been selected for publication. Why were these particular images chosen? What messages are they sending/reinforcing? Is there any author/photographer bias involved?

Application
1. 12
2. Oklahoma
3. the Red and Arkansas rivers
4. at least 8
5. 1,500
6. 1,300

Lesson 17: Charts, Graphs, and Time Lines

Reinforce students' graphing skills by having them create their own graphs based on current classroom reading in their social studies texts. If this is difficult for some learners, you can assign it as a group activity.

Application
1. The dotted line shows the manufacturer's willingness to produce widgets at different prices.
2. The solid line shows the demand for widgets at different prices.
3. the equilibrium market price
4. $3
5. They are farthest apart on the far right; this shows the greatest disparity between customers' willingness to buy widgets priced at $1 and the manufacturer's desire to produce widgets priced at $5.

Lesson 18: Chronological Order

You may want to have students practice using chronological order with material from their current social studies reading using the following activity. Divide the class into small groups; then assign different sections of either the textbook chapter students are now reading or a previous chapter. Each group should list key events from their section of the reading in chronological order. They should next scramble the events on a separate sheet of paper. These scrambled lists can be photocopied, then handed out to groups for rearranging.

Application
1. (a)—4; (b)—6; (c)—2; (d)—3; (e)—5; (f)—1
2. Answers will vary, but students should see that chronological order is a logical pattern for this sort of historical narrative to use.
3. Answers will vary, but you should help students understand that most history texts consist of straightforward historical narrative, proceeding from earlier eras to later ones. This is a logical way in which to show the evolution of cultural and political history, as well as geologic and geographic history.
4. Answers will vary.
5. Answers will vary.
6. Answers will vary, but you might remind students of the "flashback" technique, in which the story jumps back and forth between present and past.

Lesson 19: Main Idea and Details

Try quizzing students on their current social studies reading as you apply the concept of main idea versus details. Read aloud certain key statements from their social studies textbook, one by one. Students should be able to tell you whether each statement is a main idea or a detail. This can be done orally or in writing, depending on the level of formality you choose, and whether your students need the visual reinforcement of written text to facilitate their comprehension.

Application

1. (a) D   (e) D
   (b) D   (f) D
   (c) MI   (g) MI
   (d) D   (h) D
2. two
3. Topic sentence 1 is located at the very end of paragraph 1. Topic sentence 2 is located at the very beginning of paragraph 2.
4. Answers will vary, but many students may feel that it is easier to grasp the main idea when the topic sentence appears at the beginning of the paragraph.

Lesson 20: Cause and Effect

Cause and effect can often be applied to current news stories, from the results of a natural disaster to the reasons for (and fallout from) a political crisis, or the causes and results of a Wall Street panic. Using news items from the real world can help students see that the reading strategies they are learning about in class can be used every day in a meaningful context.

Application

Answers will vary.

Lesson 21: Compare and Contrast

Have students compare/contrast two world figures, two geographic regions, two political parties or ideologies, or two countries from their current social studies textbooks. These comparisons should be in written form—either informal (using a simple graphic organizer) or more formal (in carefully written paragraphs). Or, you can have students work in groups to present their information in a debate format—each group studying one side of the person, place, or issue.

Application

Answers will vary.

Part 6: Practice Readings

This section provides longer social studies selections, followed by a comprehension quiz. You may assign a particular reading strategy or allow students to choose one.

Reinforce the concept of author bias when assigning any of these readings to your students. Some of the selections are fairly straightforward narratives, but others—particularly the primary source documents—show bias.

Reading A: Dynastic Rule in Egypt

This selection is organized in chronological order. Students may find an outline or structured notes to be particularly useful strategies.

Quiz

1. (b) 2. (c) 3. (a) 4. (b) 5. (a)

Reading B: The Effect of Environment on Mesopotamian Culture

This selection is organized in a cause-and-effect pattern. A semantic web or structured notes may be the most useful strategies.

Quiz

1. (d) 2. (a) 3. (a) 4. (b) 5. (d)

Reading C: The Growth of Towns in the Middle Ages

This text follows a main-idea-and-details pattern. Any strategy works well.

Quiz

1. (a) 2. (c) 3. (d) 4. (d) 5. (b)

Reading D: Conflicting Views of Slavery

This reading presents a wonderful opportunity to discuss author bias with your students.

Quiz

1. (c) 2. (b) 3. (c) 4. (a) 5. (a)

BIBLIOGRAPY

Churchill, E. Richard, and Linda R. *Understanding Our Economy.* Revised edition. Portland, ME: J. Weston Walch, Publisher, 1998.

Churchill, E. Richard, and Linda R. *Short Lessons in U.S. History.* Portland, ME: J. Weston Walch, Publisher, 1999.

Commager, Henry Steele, and Allen Nevins, Editors. *The Heritage of America.* Revised edition. Boston: Little, Brown and Company, 1949.

Fagan, Brian. *Elusive Treasure: The Story of Early Archaeologists in the Americas.* New York: Charles Scribner's Sons, 1977.

Hilton, Kenneth. *Document-Based Assessment Activities for U.S. History Classes.* Portland, ME: J. Weston Walch, Publisher, 1999.

Levine, Ellen. *A Fence Away from Freedom: Japanese Americans and World War II.* New York: G. P. Putnam's Sons, 1995.

Microsoft Encarta Encyclopedia 1999 CD-ROM. Microsoft Corporation, 1993–1998.

Millard, Dr. Anne. *A Street Through Time: A 12,000-Year Walk Through History.* New York: DK Publishing, Inc., 1998.

Milner, Clyde A., II, Carol A. O'Connor, and Martha A. Sandweiss, Editors. *The Oxford History of the American West.* New York: Oxford University Press, 1994.

Morison, Samuel Eliot, Henry Steele Commager, and William E. Leuchtenburg. *The Growth of the American Republic, Volume One.* Seventh edition. New York: Oxford University Press, 1980.

Noonan, Theresa C. *Document-Based Assessment Activities for Global History Classes.* Portland, ME: J. Weston Walch, Publisher, 1999.

Porter, Darwin, and Danforth Prince. *Frommer's 2000: France.* New York: Macmillan General Reference USA, 2000.

Rice, Charles B. *Proceedings at the Celebration of the Two Hundredth Anniversary of First Parish at Salem Village, Now Danvers, October 8, 1872.* Boston: Congregational Publishing Society, 1874.

Sammis, Kathy. *Focus on U.S. History: The Era of Expansion and Reform.* Portland, ME: J. Weston Walch, Publisher, 1997.

Walbridge, Michael. *African-American Heroes of the Civil War.* Portland, ME: J. Weston Walch, Publisher, 2000.

Walbridge, Michael. *Latino Heroes of the Civil War.* Portland, ME: J. Weston Walch, Publisher, 1997.

Warriner, John E., Mary E. Whitten, and Francis Griffith. *English Grammar and Composition.* Revised edition. New York: Harcourt, Brace, & World, Inc., 1965.

Wilson, Wendy S., and Gerald H. Herman. *Critical Thinking Using Primary Sources in U.S. History.* Portland, ME: J. Weston Walch, Publisher, 2000.